WILD OUTSIDE

AROUND THE WORLD WITH
SURVIVORMAN

LES STROUD

ILLUSTRATIONS BY ANDREW P. BARR

annick
press

toronto · berkeley

© 2021 Stroud Publishing Inc. (text)

© 2021 Andrew P. Barr (Illustrations)

Survivorman photography by Laura Bombier

Second printing, May 2021

Pages 144 and 145 constitute an extension of this copyright page.

Cover art by Andrew P. Barr, designed by Paul Covello
Interior designed by Paul Covello
Edited by Claire Caldwell
Copyedited by Jennifer Foster
Proofread by Mary Ann Blair

Annick Press Ltd.

We acknowledge the support of the Canada Council for the Arts and the
Ontario Arts Council, and the participation of the Government of Canada/la
participation du gouvernement du Canada for our publishing activities.

Library and Archives Canada Cataloguing in Publication

Title: Wild outside : around the world with Survivorman / Les Stroud ; illustrations by Andrew P.
    Barr.
Names: Stroud, Les, author. | Barr, Andrew (Illustrator), illustrator.
Identifiers: Canadiana (print) 20200332481 | Canadiana (ebook) 2020033249X | ISBN 9781773215075
    (softcover) | ISBN 9781773215082 (HTML) | ISBN 9781773215099 (PDF) | ISBN 9781773215105 (Kindle)
Subjects: LCSH: Stroud, Les—Travel—Juvenile literature. | LCSH: Outdoor life—Juvenile literature. |
    LCSH: Outdoor recreation—Juvenile literature.
Classification: LCC GV191.62 .S77 2021 | DDC j796.5—dc23

Published in the U.S.A. by Annick Press (U.S.) Ltd.
Distributed in Canada by University of Toronto Press.
Distributed in the U.S.A. by Publishers Group West.

Printed in China

annickpress.com
lesstroud.ca
apb-art.com
laurabombier.com

Also available as an e-book.
Please visit annickpress.com/ebooks for more details.

To the kid with an adventurous heart. Is that you?
—L.S.

PART THREE: REACT

YOUR INTRODUCTION TO ADVENTURE

ONE OF MY FAVORITE PLACES TO EXPLORE WHEN I WAS GROWING UP IN MIMICO, in the west end of Toronto, Ontario, was a shallow and rocky local creek. It was behind a big hospital parking lot and underneath a highway, yet there were deer and foxes and blue herons and raccoons and bees and even some rare plants. I could pretend to be on a great wilderness adventure.

I had two heroes back then: an undersea explorer and film-maker named Jacques Cousteau and a fictional book and movie character named Tarzan the Ape Man. Because of Cousteau, I wanted to be a nature filmmaker, and because of Tarzan, I wanted to go on adventures in the jungles of the world. Eventually, I combined both of them into one person: Survivorman—aka me!

After years of training in survival, adventure, and film-making, I came up with this idea of going out into the wilderness alone and figuring out how to survive in different locations all around the world. I wanted to film those adventures, so I could show people how to survive and share in the incredible experiences I had in nature. Soon *Survivorman* became a successful show seen by millions of people. I was credited as the guy who invented a whole new type of TV program: survival TV.

As Survivorman, I have traveled more than 800,000 kilometers (half a million miles) around the globe—from the lush jungles of Papua New Guinea and the sun-scorched sands of the Kalahari Desert to the harsh cold of the Canadian north. I've caught, trapped, fished for, foraged, and cultivated wilderness food to keep my belly full. I've learned how to make a home out of leaves, vines, branches, and rocks. I've watched animals and even plants to learn how they survive.

But it all started by that creek in the city. My experiences there gave me a thirst for adventure, the "itch" to see what was around the next corner. It was also where I learned to be aware of my environment, and to work with my surroundings to solve problems and overcome challenges.

That's something everyone can do, whether in your own backyard, at a local park, or on a camping trip far into the wilderness. Learning to prepare for your journeys, observe your surroundings, react to unexpected situations, and adapt to your environment can help you have wonderful adventures closer to home and beyond. In each chapter, I'll show you how I've put these four key components of adventure—preparation, observation, reaction, and adaptation—to the test in the wilderness, and what I've learned from the natural world. You'll see what can happen when one of these components is forgotten or ignored, and what I would do differently—or not—if I could do it all over again.

You don't need to be lost in the jungle or on a deserted island to enjoy the wonder of a new experience, to discover amazing plants and animals, or to challenge yourself in the outdoors. Nature is everywhere around you. It is right outside your door.

But, if you *are* inside and you are reading this book, then be aware that each page you are about to turn is another step along an adventurous trail. You won't be alone on your adventure; I'll be right by your side. And I want you to be super prepared! Every story in this book features some of the gear I used in each situation. But there are some basic tools I like to bring on most of my adventures. So grab your survival kit, and let's go!

SURVIVORMAN'S SURVIVAL KIT

Here's my minimum kit, based on years of experience in remote wilderness and extreme conditions. Depending on the type of adventure you're going on, you may not need every piece of gear listed here. Make sure to check with an adult before handling knives, matches, or other fire-starting devices. Never use these tools alone.

In pockets or hanging from my belt:

- high-quality (sharp) belt knife and a folding knife with a saw blade
- compass
- solid matches with striker in a waterproof container
- butane lighter
- magnesium flint striker (hey—I like fires!)
- one or two large, orange garbage bags (great as signaling devices and for cover from the elements)
- metal cup (for boiling water)
- rope (parachute cord is great)
- whistle
- bottle of water

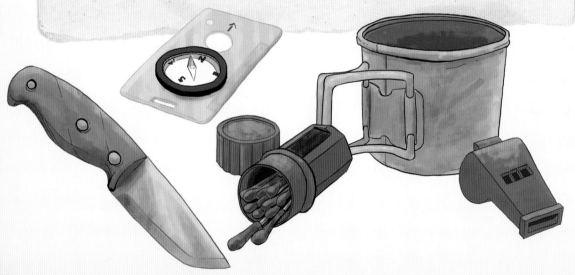

In a small kit or fanny pack (or a coffee tin with a lid, which you can also use for boiling liquid):

- dried foods (I pack enough for two days, which is about 1,800 calories per person per day. Energy bars are a great option.)
- insect screen (seasonal)
- signal mirror
- small flashlight with batteries
- snare wire
- fishing lures (three), hooks, sinkers, and line
- small folding saw
- candle
- flares

SURVIVORMAN'S TOP FIVE SURVIVAL MUST-HAVES:

1. Something to start a fire
2. A container in which to boil water
3. A form of shelter
4. A hunting or fishing device
5. Something to split wood

Before setting out on an adventure, make sure you and your adventure buddies know how to use everything in your kit!

PART ONE:
PREPARE

AS THE OLD SAYING GOES, "AN OUNCE OF PREVENTION IS WORTH A POUND OF CURE."

Benjamin Franklin, inventor and a founding father of the United States, said that. He wasn't talking about outdoor adventure, but the saying still applies. Many mistakes that can get us into real trouble in the field happen before we have even left home.

Say you're setting out on an overnight backpacking trip. Did you check the weather? Do you know what kind of terrain you'll be crossing, and how long the hike is supposed to take? Did you check to see that that old tent of yours still has all its pegs and poles, and does not leak? How about your clothing? Did you pack all the right gear?

Preparing doesn't mean you won't encounter the unexpected. The outdoors can be unpredictable. But if you take the time to prepare properly for where you are going and what you are going to do, then you stand a good chance of eliminating problems before they occur.

Good preparation can be the difference between spending the night wet and cold, or staying warm and dry. It can even be the difference between a dangerous ordeal and a good story to tell your friends later. The stories in this first chapter should help prepare you for amazing adventures, rather than leading you down a dark and dangerous trail. Are you ready?

CHAPTER 1
SLIP-SLIDING MY WAY INTO HYPOTHERMIA

ADVENTURE LOG

LOCATION: The extremely hilly Sognefjord, Norway.

CONDITIONS: At the top of the mountain, there is fluffy snow that could bury you up to your eyeballs! At the bottom, there is rain, rain, and more rain.

GEAR: Heavy winter coat and pants, and, as always, my trusty camera.

MISSION: Trek to the bottom of a mountain, where one wrong move could mean slipping off a towering cliff—and not moving at all would mean freezing.

WHEN I CONSIDERED MY CLIMB DOWN THE HILL, I THOUGHT, *No problem. I've climbed down hundreds of mountains and hills. This will be a walk in the park.* I couldn't have been more wrong.

There is really only one attitude that gets me in trouble when I am out in the wilderness, and it always starts the same way. I have a day or an hour or just a moment when I become overconfident. I'm not paying attention. I think nothing can go wrong.

This is a very dangerous way to think.

I had just spent four and a half days stuck inside a car. I was bogged down by snow on a deserted mountain road, where I was filming my latest episode of *Survivorman*. That's a miserable place to be! I was cold and hungry. After more than four days, my survival supplies that came with the car's emergency kit were running out. Now I had to head downhill toward the ocean fjord, where I could find edible wild plants to eat.

But I hadn't brought a map. Someone had given me directions before I began filming, and I figured I would remember them. Wrong. *No problem*, I thought again. *I'll just make my way down, straight through the forest.* Big mistake.

The mountain was so steep, it felt more like I was *climbing* downhill than hiking. Think of a tobogganing hill, only steeper. My legs plunged into waist-deep snow with every step. The thick trees made it hard to see the terrain ahead. I was guessing my way down the mountain.

It began to snow heavily. Everywhere I looked was a wall of big, fat white flakes blowing fiercely in the mountain winds. They stung my watering eyes.

HOW I CREATE SURVIVAL STORIES

For my television series, I would often film survival scenarios that could happen to anyone, including you! They are simple ordeals, like getting lost on a hiking trail. I really enjoy simulating these real-life experiences and filming my survival techniques to show people how to self-rescue. For every scenario, I highlight a different set of survival skills, such as fire-starting or shelter-building. For my survival ordeal in Norway, I stuck myself in a small car near the top of a snowy and blowy mountain. I wanted to show viewers how to get warm in cold conditions.

As I got lower on the mountain and the air warmed up, this fluffy snow turned to wet flakes that stuck to me. Then it turned to freezing rain. My heavy winter coat was soaked right through. I knew that I could encounter these conditions on the mountain, yet I didn't pack a raincoat due to my overconfidence. Now that I was in this situation, staying put and waiting for better weather would've been the smartest thing to do. But I was impatient to get down to the ocean for a better chance at finding food. Impatience is the wrong kind of motivator in a tough situation.

After a few hours, my legs were so tired they felt like rubber. People tend to think going uphill is tougher than going downhill, but it's not. Although you might get out of breath faster going uphill, going downhill is harder on your muscles. You have to pay close attention to where you put your feet, so you stay balanced and don't fall. I should've prepared better at home by exercising my legs to get them ready for Norway's steep terrain.

NORWAY

Norway is a country in northwestern Europe, with coasts on the North Atlantic Ocean and the Barents Sea. The fjords of Norway are long narrow bays jutting inland from the ocean. The moisture keeps the lower lands green and free of snow. Norway has more than 1,500 fjords!

I started to sweat. I was sweating so much that the clothing close to my skin became as wet as my outer layers. I had to sit down often to rest. I even slid down steep sections of the mountain on my butt. However, this was not a fun day of tobogganing. This was really scary! My pants were getting torn to shreds.

PREPARE

The best way to dress for winter temperatures is to wear layers of clothing you can take off and put back on again. Practice the art of layering, so you don't get sweaty or cold.

During the day it may feel fine to build up body heat while working hard. In the winter it even feels good to get nice and warm while we work or play in the snow. But if you work too hard, you may begin to sweat. As night comes or when you stop exercising, being wet from sweat will make you very chilled. You could even become hypothermic. You must stay dry. As I always say, you sweat, you die!

As the sunlight began to fade, I thought it couldn't get any worse. But it did. I slid to a stop above cliffs covered in ice. Behind me was a steep, wet, snow-covered trail. I'd never be able to climb back up. I was about to get trapped on the side of the mountain.

TRY THIS AT HOME

Tracking weather patterns can help you prepare to head outside with the right gear and clothing. Want to learn more about weather patterns in your neighborhood? Make a rain gauge at home.

Items needed:

- office tape or clear tape
- pair of scissors
- craft knife
- ruler
- piece of paper (8 by 11 inches)
- black permanent marker
- piece of dowel, 20 centimeters (eight inches) long, or cut off the end of a broomstick
- modeling clay
- plastic bottle

1. Wrap your paper around the bottle about two-thirds from the bottom. Draw a line around the bottle with your marker, using the paper as a guide.

2. Remove the paper and ask an adult to help you cut around the bottle, along this black line.

3. Place the modeling clay in the bottom of the bottle and use the broom stick to push the clay down until it forms a flat base. Get rid of all the air gaps.

4. Tape the ruler to the inside of the bottle, with the measurements starting from the bottom. You may need to push the ruler down into the clay.

5. Take the top of the bottle, remove the cap, and set the top upside down in the upper part of the bottle (where you just put the ruler). It will fit snugly and will keep things like leaves out of the water.

6. Finally, position your rain gauge outside in the open, where nothing will stop the rain from falling into the top. Check each day how deep the water is on the ruler, and write down your results. Don't forget to empty the gauge every day, so you are starting from scratch for your day's measurement.

There was only one thing I could do while there was still daylight. I could stop, rest, and seriously think about the danger I was in. That's right. Thinking is actually something you can do. I concentrated hard on my options. I might not have prepared well for this adventure, but I could take a moment now to prepare for the rest of my journey down to the fjord. My overconfidence had evaporated somewhere on the side of the mountain. No more impatience for me. My humility, my better sense, had finally made me sit down and take my time to figure out what to do.

I knew I couldn't spend the night in this rain and snow because I would slip into hypothermia. That is what happens when your body can't keep itself warm anymore. It can be very dangerous. Eventually, getting that cold can kill you.

Feeling very embarrassed, even though no one was there to make fun of me, I sat on my butt and inched my way toward the green fjords. The mountain had beaten me, so I showed it my respect by slowing myself down and humbly sliding to the bottom on my butt.

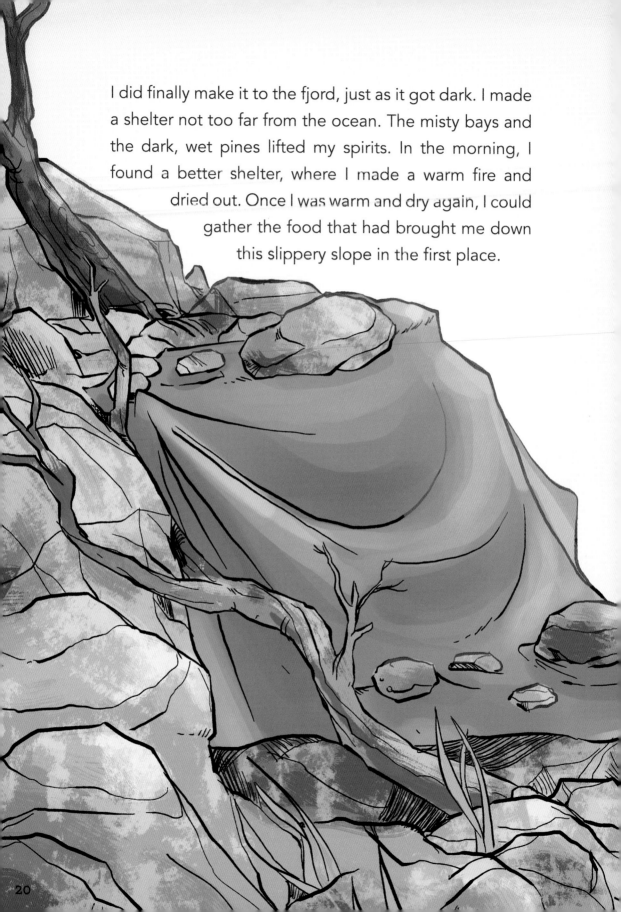

I did finally make it to the fjord, just as it got dark. I made a shelter not too far from the ocean. The misty bays and the dark, wet pines lifted my spirits. In the morning, I found a better shelter, where I made a warm fire and dried out. Once I was warm and dry again, I could gather the food that had brought me down this slippery slope in the first place.

MISSION ACCOMPLISHED?

Well, sort of. I was too casual about my pre-adventure research. I assumed I could handle whatever was thrown at me. Preparing by bringing a map would have made my trip down the mountain much quicker and safer.

I also might have thought to bring a raincoat! Once in the dangerous situation, I should have humbled myself to the circumstances much sooner than I did.

I could've died on the side of a mountain because of poor preparation and planning. I made it, but I could've avoided a lot of the fear and risk—and saved a pair of pants—if I'd been more on the ball.

CHAPTER 2
HIGH-SPEED MOOSE CHASE

ADVENTURE LOG

LOCATION: A remote, swampy forest shore well away from the main canoeing routes in Algonquin Provincial Park, Ontario, Canada.

CONDITIONS: Early fall, warm and sunny, though the morning had started with frost on the ground.

GEAR: Canoe and sturdy, fall-weather clothing for bushwhacking (off-trail hiking in the woods).

MISSION: Say hello to a moose couple and then try to get out of the forest alive!

I WAS HIKING BACK TO MY CANOE WHEN I NOTICED HER

—a big, beautiful cow moose, gently eating lily pads in a pond, up to her belly in the murky water. She gracefully dipped her big nose deep into the water and came up munching the swamp flowers. Mud and water drizzled off her brown, hairy chin. I had not startled her when I came noisily hiking through the pine and birch trees, scrambling over and around stumps and branches. This was odd behavior. Why wouldn't she run away? They usually do. Most animals run away from humans. But there we stood, only six meters (20 feet) from each other—her eating lazily, while I watched in amazement with a big goofy grin on my face.

Six meters in front of a moose can be a dangerous place to stand, especially if there are calves nearby. Moose mothers can be extremely protective of their young and might chase you away. A moose is as big and strong as any horse you may have seen, and like horses, their hard, heavy hooves can be dangerous—even deadly.

TRY THIS AT HOME

Like most maps, topographical maps (or "topos") show you where to find forests, lakes, rivers, and even small creeks and streams. Topos also show you how rugged and hilly the ground is. Topographical maps are a great tool to help you prepare for an outdoor adventure and find the best routes through the wilderness—especially if there are no marked trails. You can search online for topographical maps of your neighborhood. See if you can find your own address and then look for any nature areas that are close by. Or go high tech and use Google Earth to locate your home. Make sure you switch it to "satellite" view, so you can see the forests or green patches.

PREPARE

Checklists are the simplest way to prepare for an adventure. Before heading out, write up simple lists of things to do, things to check, and things to pack for your excursion. Don't leave the house until you have checked off everything on your lists.

Here's an example of what you could include on a checklist:

- Pack survival kit.
- Pack first aid kit and replace any supplies as needed.
- Pack any special gear needed for the trip (for example, snowshoes for winter travel).
- Check the weather and dress/pack clothes for those conditions.
- Check clothes for holes, rips, or any other issues (like a jammed zipper), and repair/replace as needed.
- Plan route and pack map or GPS tracker.
- Tell someone where I'm going, what I'm doing, and when I plan to be back.
- Set a time for this person to call for help if they haven't heard from me.
- Pack enough food and water for the adventure.

As I stood there, I realized I had made a classic adventuring mistake before I had even left home. I had researched my route using topographical maps—that was good. But I hadn't made any other plans. That was bad. I hadn't bothered to take my trusty survival kit with me. That was really bad. I had paddled far from the main canoeing routes. And I hadn't told anyone where I was going or when I planned to be back. That was really, *really* bad.

When the unexpected happens, like bumping into a big moose in the middle of the forest, you want to know someone at home has your back. Today, though, no one would know to come looking for me if I got into trouble.

But since the cow seemed to be alone, I stayed there and enjoyed our moment together. *What could go wrong? I thought.*

It was so enjoyable that I decided I would try to talk to her. In moose-speak. Cow moose and bull moose (males) make different sounds. A bull will grunt over and over with a deep, low bark. Cows will let out a long, high-pitched whine. I thought to myself, *If I do a bull sound, I might scare her off. Or even worse, I might anger some nearby bull moose. He would think I was stealing his girlfriend.* This was the "season of love," after all. Every fall, bulls and cows get together to mate and make babies, which would be born in the spring.

A cow sound seemed like a safer way to say "Hello." I made one call. She looked up at me for a second, then she went back to eating. I made a second call. She didn't even bother to look up. Maybe I was boring her.

ALL ABOUT ANTLERS

Bull moose spend most of the year preparing for mating season by growing their antlers. When they first start to grow, the antlers are covered with a soft layer of "velvet," which is made up of blood vessels. These vessels carry food to the antlers, to make them grow large and strong. In the early autumn the velvet falls off, and bulls use their antlers to battle each other for the affections of the female moose. Talk about a major headache! The antlers fall off after mating season, and the whole cycle starts again.

I would have loved to spend more time with the moose, but the sun was setting, and I needed to go home. I took one step to leave . . . and out jumped a huge bull moose with a rack of antlers big enough to push over a car! He was even *bigger* than most horses you might have seen.

He had been hiding in the thick trees right beside the calm and quiet cow, and she was his date. He was looking right at me with big, red, bulging eyes. He snorted, grunted, then charged toward me at full speed.

With my heart pumping hard, I ran and ran and ran. I saw a tree I knew I could climb and scrambled up its trunk about 4.5 meters (15 feet) off the ground. But the bull wasn't done chasing me. He stood below the tree grunting and stomping and breaking smaller trees. Why was he so angry at little ol' me?

Moose have huge ears and excellent hearing. If you cup your hands behind your ears, you can get an idea of how things sound to a moose.

Then I understood. "D'oh!" I grunted as I slapped my forehead. I had imitated a female moose call. Maybe he wasn't chasing me away from his girlfriend. Maybe he was falling in love with me?

It was getting really dark, and I didn't want to be stuck up in this tree all night, shivering in the cold autumn temperatures. And what if I grew tired and lost my grip? I'd fall to the ground. *No one even knows I'm out here*, I thought nervously.

After 15 minutes, the moose backed away slightly. That was my chance. I jumped down and ran toward my canoe. He started chasing me again. I made it to the water's edge, but I was still a long way from my canoe, and I had to catch my breath. I hid behind a tree and stayed as quiet as possible. The moose seemed to slow down, and I realized he couldn't tell where I was. He had been following the loud sounds I was making while I ran, using his hearing—rather than his eyesight—to locate me.

There was only one way to sneak away from this big bull. I slipped into the cold lake. With just my head above the surface, I floated along the shoreline, making not a single sound. I glided past a snow bunting sitting on a branch close to the water. She must have thought, *Humans are so weird*. Once I made it to my canoe, I jumped inside, soaking wet, and paddled away as fast as I could. There was no way I was going to be some moose's girlfriend!

MISSION ACCOMPLISHED?

Sort of. Being chased by the moose just happened. Pure chance. But my lack of preparation made the situation more dangerous than it needed to be.

If I had told someone where I was going, I wouldn't have felt so alone and so desperate to run out of the forest and away from the moose—and I might not have risked hypothermia by jumping in the cold lake. If I had brought along my survival kit, I would've had some good survival gear if I really did get stuck up in that tree all night. With a satellite phone, I could've called someone to let them know of my situation. I reacted the best way I could, but I also got lucky.

Getting lucky certainly happens in survival situations, but you can't count on it. And being well-prepared lowers the chances that you'll have to rely on luck at all.

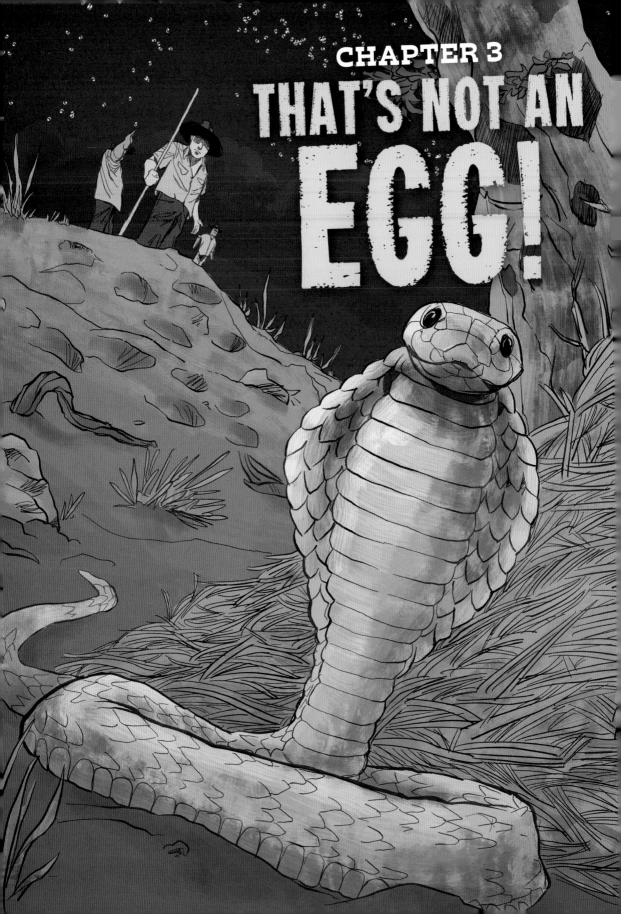

CHAPTER 3
THAT'S NOT AN EGG!

ADVENTURE LOG

LOCATION: The Kalahari Desert, Namibia, Africa. Think massive, scarlet-colored sand dunes broken up by rocky, sandy scrubland—with no water in sight.

CONDITIONS: Imagine the hottest you have ever felt. Now think of that being five times worse! During the day, the hot winds blow every last drop of moisture away from your body and leave you feeling like a dry, crumpled leaf. Sand gets in every nook and cranny of your clothing and skin, and makes you itchy and sore. But at night, it gets cold enough to make you shiver.

GEAR: Snake pole with a "grip trigger" and a flashlight.

MISSION: Trek through the desert to learn how to find weaverbird eggs . . . or risk going hungry on my weeklong survival ordeal.

WHAT IS THE BEST WAY TO LEARN ADVENTURE AND SURVIVAL SKILLS? It's heading out with an expert who can show you the methods that will make for the best time ever.

I had read books about the Kalahari Desert to prepare for my survival mission there, but spending time on the land with experts would make a huge difference in how well I would do on my own. So I did some extensive online research and found Douw and Rick, survival experts with experience in the southern half of Africa, including countries such as South Africa, Namibia, Botswana, and Kenya.

They agreed to meet me in Namibia. They also connected me with Raphael, a local San Bushman guide they knew, who would join us on this exploratory expedition. This is how I found myself crossing huge red sand dunes with three guides on a dark desert night, looking for weaverbirds and their eggs.

LEAVE NOTHING TO CHANCE!

Some people think I just hop on a plane and drop into a desert, jungle, or forest to survive. It's never that simple. I do my research first. I search online to find local folks who could take me out and teach me survival methods. I read books about wild edible plants, dangerous critters, the local weather, and even what to wear in the area. Every mountain, jungle, and desert (like the Kalahari, pictured here) is different, so there is always something new to learn. For *Survivorman*, I would usually spend about five days training and preparing on location before I headed out on my own to film myself surviving for seven days.

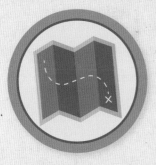

PREPARE

When you search online for experts who offer classes in adventure and survival, it's important not to just pick the first one you find. Lots of people like to teach these skills, but not everyone has the years of experience needed to be a good teacher. Look for reviews of the teacher and the courses they offer.

One trick I used to use when contacting someone who claimed experience in survival was to ask if they knew much about edible wild plants. This often seems to be the last skill people learn when training in adventure and survival. I reasoned that if they knew the wild plants of their region, they would likely be good at lots of other skills, too.

Earlier in the day, Raphael had shown me which plants would have juice I could squeeze out to drink. Now he wanted to show me how to get a more substantial meal. So Raphael, Douw, Rick, and I shone our flashlights up and down the dunes, trying to spot one of the birds' huge, funnel-shaped nests. We had to search at night because during the day, weaverbirds leave their nests to get food. We could've found eggs at any time, but at night, we also had the chance to catch a bird. You can eat a weaverbird just like you'd eat chicken. Meat can help you stay alive in a tough survival situation, so it was important I learn this survival trick.

Finally, Raphael's flashlight beam landed on a massive, dry grass nest hanging almost a meter (three feet) off the ground. Slowly we crept toward it, trying not to make a sound. Raphael crawled underneath and asked me to do the same. He pointed at the hole I'd need to shove my arm into to try and catch a bird or find an egg. He decided he'd better show me how it was done.

TRY THIS AT HOME

Weaverbirds aren't the only ones who build nests with an entrance at the bottom, though most are much smaller than the ones I saw in the Kalahari.

To find out about birds that make funnel nests, check out a guidebook or do online research about birds in your area. Once you find out who is living nearby, arrange an outing with an experienced birdwatcher and try to spot the funnel nests in your neighborhood.

If you think gathering weaverbird eggs sounds dangerous, wait until you hear about ostrich eggs (pictured above). These eggs are huge—about the equivalent of eight chicken eggs, or the size of a softball. You can walk up to a nest on the ground and pick them up. But beware: an ostrich can be up to 2.7 meters (nine feet) tall, weigh up to 45 kilograms (100 pounds), kick as hard as a horse, and run as fast as a car. Ostriches have even killed lions! With their 10-centimeter-long (four-inch-long) talons, they're the most dangerous bird on the planet.

Raphael reached in all the way to his elbow. Then he got a strange look on his face—something was wrong. He reached around a little more, then his eyes widened, and he yanked his arm out. He jumped back with a shriek, and so did I. He started talking nonstop in his San language. Douw translated. He told me Raphael hadn't felt any birds or eggs.

What he *had* felt was the body of a large Cape cobra snake!

SSSSTAY AWAY FROM THAT SNAKE!

The Cape cobra, also called the yellow cobra, is not very aggressive compared to other venomous snakes in Africa. If it feels threatened, it will usually try to get away—fast. But if it has no escape route, it might strike. Without treatment, a Cape cobra bite can kill a person in half an hour. It's not so easy to take snakebite medicine, called antivenom, on an adventure. For starters, it has to be kept cold. Then you need special training to administer it: give too much and it can kill someone; give too little and it won't save them from the bite. Plus, one vial of antivenom can cost more than a thousand dollars, and there are dozens of varieties for different types of snakebites.

This beautiful but deadly African snake also likes to eat weaverbirds and their eggs, and it will sometimes use their nests as a home. We all backed away, but not before I shone my flashlight up inside the hole to see the snake. I even filmed it.

Rick, who happened to be a snake expert, got so excited about this discovery that he pulled out his snake pole—a 1.5-meter (five-foot) rod with a special hook on the end. He pushed the pole up into the nest, promising to show us the snake. Well, the rest of us weren't so sure we wanted to see one of the most deadly snakes in the world up close, so we scrambled out of the way.

SNAKE COUNTRY

If you're hiking somewhere with snakes, carry a long stick. You can use it to defend yourself if you surprise a snake in the grass or among rocks. It can also help to take heavy steps. Snakes will feel the ground rumbling as you stomp and will often slither out of your way. You might never know one was right in front of you!

After a moment or two, he pulled the 1.5-meter-long (five-foot-long) golden-colored Cape cobra out of the nest. It fell with a *thud*, then started to slither across the sand. We all ran up the sand dune to higher ground—except Rick. He calmly and casually turned the snake around using his snake pole and sent him on his way in a different direction from the nest—and us.

All of a sudden, I wasn't so sure I was going to be hungry for weaverbird eggs anytime soon. This nighttime expedition hadn't just prepared me for how to find food in the Kalahari. It also showed me I might have some dangerous competition for my next meal!

MISSION ACCOMPLISHED?

Yes. By spending some time with local experts, I was better prepared for the week that lay ahead of me in the desert.

Later, when I was alone, I remembered to poke a stick into a nest I'd found before reaching inside with my hand. Once I made sure there were no snakes, only birds, I was free to safely grab some eggs to eat.

PART TWO:

OBSERVE

WHERE ARE YOU RIGHT NOW? Are you sitting on the floor or your bed or a chair? Maybe you're reading outside— good choice! What do you hear? What do you smell? Is it hot, cold, or just perfect? Noticing (observing) what is going on all around you helps you to be aware of dangers. Can you relax because everything is calm and quiet? Or do you need to move somewhere else because it's too noisy to concentrate? You can observe big things, like the weather. Maybe it's raining outside, so you should stay in and keep reading. Or you can notice smaller things—like maybe you're uncomfortable because you're sitting on a pen.

When facing a dangerous or challenging situation on an adventure, you never want to guess at what you need to do. You want to make the best decision you can, based on the

information you have. If you haven't observed what has just happened, what's happening right this second, and what is all around you, then you're closing your eyes to all the possibilities available to you. If you're not in a crisis, good observation can help you avoid trouble . . . and lead to delightful surprises on any adventure. So take one more look around, get comfy, and read on.

ADVENTURE LOG

LOCATION: A bush trail in Temagami, Ontario, Canada— my home for many years.

CONDITIONS: A warm and sunny spring day. The birds were chirping. The mosquitos were biting. The air was fresh and clear. The lakes and rivers were full of water from the snow melt and the spring rains.

GEAR: Three of my five senses (sight, hearing, and smell) to notice everything around me while I jogged, a good pair of trail-running shoes, a small backpack full of groceries.

MISSION: A mysterious creature moves through the bushes, coming closer with every step. I must determine if I should run, or stand perfectly still and let it walk on by.

THE ANIMAL CAME CLOSER AND CLOSER. I held my breath and tried not to move a muscle. I listened as it crept through the swamp plants, out of sight. Soon, the creature would come right up onto the trail.

I had been jogging through the forest, when I rounded a corner and came upon a pretty swamp filled with cattails. I paused. I was carrying a week's worth of groceries on my back, but I was tempted to pick a few cattails, too. At this time of year, they're really tasty!

Then, I'd noticed something. The cattails were moving. Something was walking through them, making their long stalks wave in the air.

I stood very, very still and tried to guess what it might be by the way it was walking and the soft, gentle sound its steps made in the water. It was only about 12 meters (40 feet) from me, and I didn't want to scare the mystery animal. I wanted to get a good look at it. As soon as I knew what I was dealing with, I could figure out the safest move

North America's boreal forest, also called the taiga, spans the northern part of the continent from Alaska to Newfoundland, and covers an astonishing six million square kilometers (1.5 billion acres). That's larger than most countries. Temagami is located in the Great Lakes/boreal forest crossover region. This means two kinds of forest meet each other, leading to unique scenery that exists nowhere else on the planet.

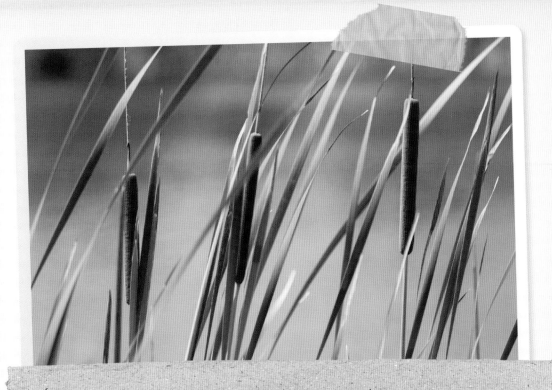

CATTAILS: NATURE'S SUPERMARKET

This plant got this nickname because you can eat almost every part of it at different times of the year—and you usually find lots of cattails in one place. The bottom ends of the stalks can be peeled and eaten raw in the spring and taste like celery mixed with cucumber. You can munch the big, hot dog–like top just as you would corn on the cob in the early summer, and the seeds can be turned into flour to make delicious bread.

to make. Running away could signal to a big predator, like a bear or a cougar, that I was a prey animal—something they might want to eat. I thought this creature might be a bear cub that had wandered away from its mother, so I peered into the bush for signs of a protective—and potentially dangerous—mama bear. Or maybe it was a small wolf hunting for squirrels. In this moment the best thing I could do was stay still, watch, and wait.

A second later, a beautiful Canadian lynx popped out of the cattails, only one meter (three feet) in front of me.

This cat was young and on the smaller side for a lynx. Since I was much bigger than her, I knew she would be more scared of me than I should be of her. I remained calm. I didn't flinch. This was a rare and wonderful opportunity to safely encounter wildlife. I didn't want to miss this amazing moment!

TRY THIS AT HOME

Many wildlife encounters happen close to home. Even in big North American cities, large wildlife such as deer, coyotes, and cougars can roam through "greenbelts" that connect the city to wild areas beyond. You might also see owls, foxes, porcupines, skunks, weasels, and raccoons. In Mumbai, India, leopards have been known to prowl the streets!

Search online or stop by a local nature store or center to find out what animals (and reptiles and birds and insects and other creatures) live near you, then head out and try to find signs of them.

A lynx is a wild cat that lives mostly in the boreal forest. Bigger than house cats, lynx can grow as big as a border collie. They stay active all year round, as their big padded feet are perfect for walking on snow in the winter. Their favorite food is snowshoe hare, a larger relative of rabbits.

When she saw me, she froze. Then she seemed to calm down. I could see in her relaxed eyes that she wasn't afraid. Her fur was not standing up on the back of her neck (even a pet cat will do this if it is angry or upset). It seemed she knew I wasn't going to hurt her. Ever so slowly, she started to walk toward me. She came so close I could have touched her, but I didn't move. Her little nostrils wiggled as she tried to figure out what I was by smelling me. Then she turned to walk away.

OBSERVE

What to do when you encounter wildlife:

- Remain calm and stand still—don't run away!
- Observe the animal's body language. If an animal's hair is sticking up, it is most likely upset.
- Take a sniff. You can sometimes smell when an animal is stressed or angry. This happens to humans, too. We sweat when we're nervous or upset, and boy, does it stink.
- Listen to the animal. Is it growling, barking, or hissing? Maybe it's chomping its teeth. Those are clear signs to get out of its way cautiously but quickly.

Now, I don't always do the right thing when I am alone in the forest. As you have already heard, I once called out to a cow moose and then got chased by her 690-kilogram (1,500-pound) boyfriend (see Chapter 2). Then there was the time I walked too close to a baby elk and its mother chased me for 274 meters (300 yards). But because this was a young, relaxed animal with no babies, I decided to take a chance. I bent down and called to her with short kisses, just like you might call your cat at home.

I couldn't believe my eyes. This beautiful lynx heard me, turned back around, and came close enough to sniff my fingers. I moved my hand slowly, so as not to frighten her away. She took one more sniff and disappeared back into the forest.

MISSION ACCOMPLISHED?

Definitely! Observations I made in the moment and earlier in the summer helped make this one of the best wildlife encounters I've ever had.

I had memorized the trail's twists and turns, in case I had to make a quick getaway. I hadn't seen any bear or cougar poop, which made me pretty confident there weren't too many large predators in the area. Just in case, I watched how the cattails moved to see how big the animal might be. A large animal would've pushed the cattails right over, but these ones swayed gently.

Finally, I knew I was in no danger by observing the lynx closely. She didn't seem stressed or aggressive. Noticing all the signs that things were safe allowed me to relax and enjoy the experience. If I had not observed what was going on, I might have reacted too quickly by running away and then I would've missed the chance to meet this wild little kitty.

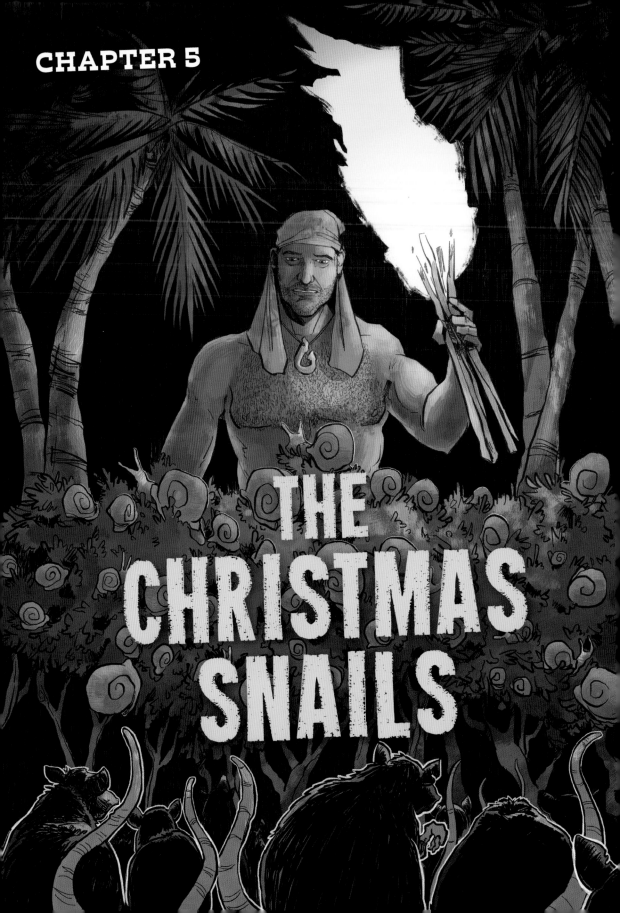

CHAPTER 5

ADVENTURE LOG

LOCATION: Cook Islands, South Pacific Ocean. A tiny, uninhabited island in the middle of the ocean. A tropical paradise.

CONDITIONS: Perfect beach weather: sunny and hot. Although I had to find food and fresh water, my only other challenge was getting sand out from between my toes!

GEAR: My dive gear, including fins and mask; my harmonica, to keep me company; a dive knife.

MISSION: Figure out why the snails were acting so strange on this small tropical island. Did their weird behavior mean I was in danger?

I ADJUSTED MY MASK ONE LAST TIME AND JUMPED INTO THE OCEAN. By the time I surfaced, my boat was already speeding away, leaving me behind. Just above the waves, I could see the island where I would spend the next seven days filming an episode of *Survivorman*. I swam toward it, wondering what mysteries this tropical paradise might hold.

But as I reached the shore, I remembered that I was in the middle of a survival ordeal. I was alone and stranded. Though this island seemed like the perfect place to take a beach vacation, I needed to take stock of my surroundings to ensure I would safely make it through the week.

I watched an ocean bird dart across the bright blue sky. Occasionally, it dove straight into the seawater, only to come up victoriously with a small fish in its beak. This told me I should go snorkeling to catch my own fish. I noticed the tide creeping up the beach. This told me where to build my shelter, so I would stay dry. I heard the loud *thud* of a coconut falling from its tree. This told me where I could find an easy meal.

But that night, I noticed something I couldn't explain at all: long, winding lines in the sand that led to the nearest shrub. What might have made these tracks? Snakes? Little birds? Gigantic worms? Then I noticed that the bushes looked like they were decorated with small gray Christmas ornaments (funnily enough, it was actually December). I moved in closer and discovered that they were snails! Hundreds of small gray snails clinging to the tops of the shrubs. *Snails certainly don't do this in my neighborhood. They are supposed to stay on the ground*, I thought.

The Cook Islands, a country in the South Pacific Ocean, is made up of 15 islands—three of them with no inhabitants—and two reefs.

I puzzled and puzzled over this, but I could not figure out why all these silly snails would climb to the tops of shrubs just before dark. Did they know something I didn't? What if their strange activities were a sign of something more sinister that could affect me? *Maybe the tide will come up this far and I might drown in my sleep*, I thought. *Maybe big snakes come out at night, and the snails climb the bushes to stay out of their reach.* Finding out why the snails were doing this could prove important for my own survival.

TRY THIS AT HOME

A blind is a structure where you can hide and watch wild creatures— without them seeing you! Follow these steps to make your own blind and become a secret wildlife detective.

Materials:

- old tent
- black marker
- spray paint (green/black/brown)
- scissors

1. Set up the tent and crawl inside.
2. Think of all the places, other than the windows, you might want to peek through to observe animals in their habitat. Use a black marker to draw all those spots on the inside of the tent fabric. Make them just big enough to look through, or to stick a camera lens through.
3. With an adult's help, cut three sides of a square in these places, going through both the inside and the outside layers, leaving the top uncut, so the fabric hangs down like a flap.

On my fifth night, I had had a particularly good day of catching clams and finding coconuts, so I was having a feast. Since it took me a while to cook my food, I stayed up much later than I had on the other nights that week. I kept a fire going well into the night and relaxed in the evening air, nibbling on my tasty tropical treats like I was on vacation.

All of a sudden, I heard something scurry past. Then it happened again. Whatever these animals were, they seemed to be the size of a squirrel. They were as fast as squirrels, too. Again and again, they ran past, too fast for me to see clearly. I squinted into the darkness, wondering if these creatures were drawn to the fire or my food. Then one animal hit my foot and jumped high in the air.

4. On the outside of the tent, spray-paint a camouflage pattern in green, black, and brown.

5. If the tent comes with a rain fly, leave that at home—you won't need it. We'll plan this for sunny days. If you want the blind to be even lighter when you carry it, you can cut out the bottom.

6. Set up the blind near the edge of a marsh or forest or field. You can throw some branches and grass on the top and sides of the tent to make it look extra "earthy."

7. Climb inside the tent. You may not see anything at first, but the longer you sit quietly, hidden in your blind, the more likely it is that wildlife will come near. You will be amazed by what you might see. Once, when I was just getting started in my filmmaking career, I went to a small island in the middle of Lake Superior and filmed a whole herd of caribou that stopped to eat a few feet away from my blind!

Rats! Dozens of big, furry rats. I hadn't noticed them before because I was usually asleep by this time, with all my food put away.

These must be Captain Cook's rats, I realized. The Cook Islands are named for Captain James Cook, an explorer who traveled the world by sea in the 1700s, coming ashore in hundreds of places he'd never seen before. He accidentally left behind rats, mice, cats, and birds that had snuck aboard his ships during his journeys.

These rats were the descendants of stowaways that hid out on Cook's ship and swam to the islands when he was moored close by. Yes, rats can swim. Especially when they smell fresh water and food.

OBSERVE

I have always loved observing wildlife. As a kid, I discovered all kinds of exciting worlds by turning over rocks and rotten logs and peeking around in the tall grass. I constructed my own animal blinds so I could stay hidden, yet close to bigger animals and birds while they went about their lives. Try observing creatures that live in your area. You can record their behaviors in a notebook to track their habits—or anything unusual. And don't forget to post your pictures online. You'd be surprised how many hashtags exist for the animals you may discover.

For the rest of the night, these Captain Cook rats scampered around me. A few even ran right across my legs. The light from my fire allowed me to watch their silly antics. And then I noticed something more. The rats were jumping up and trying to grab the snails. These clever snails had adapted to hundreds of years of being attacked and eaten by rats. They'd learned that if they climbed up the small shrubs at dusk, they could hang on branches just out of the rats' reach. What an amazing bit of clever thinking. In scientific study, this kind of reaction might be called a learned response, or maybe a biological solution due to natural selection. But I just call it very smart snails!

Once, the snails lived here without having to worry about rats eating them. Then the rats arrived. Both the local species (the snails) and the invasive species (the rats) had to change their behavior or die. The snails had to avoid being eaten by the rats, and the rats would starve if they didn't learn to catch the snails! Over hundreds of years, these two species worked out a new predator-prey relationship that would ensure both species' survival on the island. The higher the snails climbed on the shrubs, the less likely a rat could jump high enough to grab them. And I got to observe it all while I sat by my fire eating coconuts.

AVOIDING HITCHHIKING SPECIES!

While the snails and rats found a balance on that one tiny island, invasive species can be a big problem. For example, invasive Burmese pythons, Nile monitor lizards (like the one pictured above), and other creatures now live in the Florida Everglades after escaping from home aquariums. These animals are killing endangered species in the area and stealing food from other big predators.

You can help keep the number of invasive species down by traveling smart:

- Before you pack, empty your suitcase and shake it out. You might be shocked by what's been hiding inside. I have seen spiders and beetles and even a snake tumble out!

- If possible, leave your suitcase outside in the cold when you get home from warmer countries. If any tiny organisms have stowed away, they will likely die overnight.

- Rinse off the soles of your shoes before you get on a plane, especially if you have been walking in mud, sand, or grass.

- Never purposely bring home any type of creature, no matter how small.

- Never release a pet from a store into the wild.

Although the snails' behavior didn't end up affecting my survival, watching them taught me something valuable about the ecology of the island. There may have not been any snow. There may not have been any Santa Claus. There may not have been any presents. But these snails decorating the shrubs like Christmas trees made sure I had a merry Christmas just the same!

MISSION ACCOMPLISHED?

Yes. When you carefully and patiently observe the creatures all around you, one mystery leads to another until you discover an answer.

I've watched a lot of snails, so I knew hanging off the leaves of shrubs was not a normal activity for them. They usually crawl along the ground. It's possible that they have always done this on the Cook Islands, but through observing them closely and watching the rats, I guessed that this was a learned response to the threat of being eaten. It shows you how intelligent even a creature as small as a snail can be!

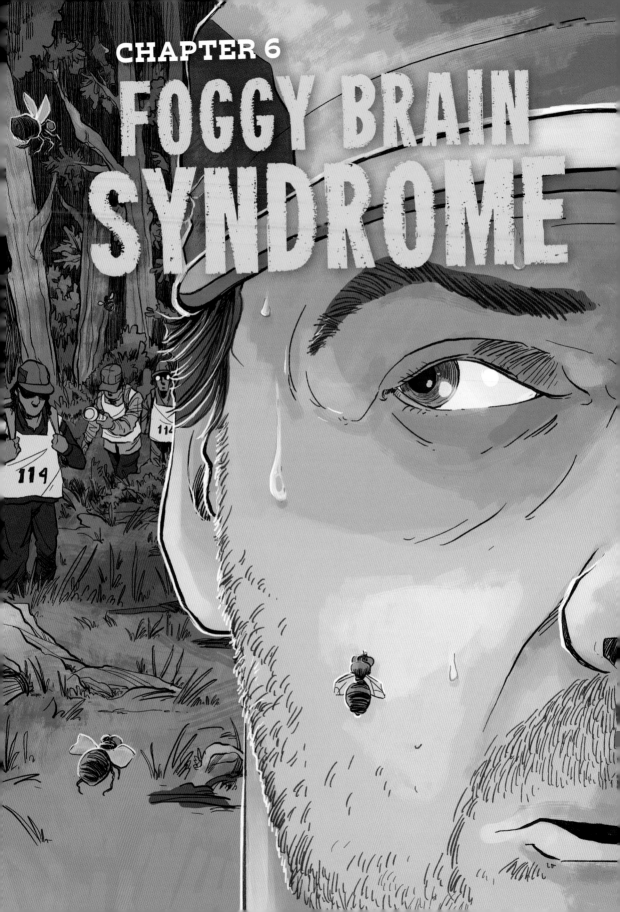

CHAPTER 6
FOGGY BRAIN SYNDROME

ADVENTURE LOG

LOCATION: Thick boreal forest near Timmins, Ontario, Canada.

CONDITIONS: Humid enough to make you sweat without moving. Buggy enough to make you horribly itchy unless you kept moving!

GEAR: Small backpack with energy bars for quick nutrition, compass, topographical map.

MISSION: Navigate (in the dark) out of the thick northern forest with my three teammates during the Canadian Adventure Racing Championship.

OUR TEAM OF FOUR HAD BEEN RUNNING FOR TWO WHOLE DAYS AND NIGHTS. We were hot and sweaty, and swollen up with mosquito and blackfly bites. Our flashlights lit up the thick bush ahead as we struggled through the darkness.

I was with my friends Tina, Steve, and Doug, and there was no stopping. Once or twice, we rested on the bare ground for a few minutes of sleep. But we had to get up and keep running—or fall behind in the race!

BLACKFLIES BITE, MOSQUITOS SUCK

During this race, the blackflies would not leave us alone for a second. Unlike a mosquito that sucks your blood through a long tube called a proboscis, the tiny blackfly will bite out a chunk of your skin! I have had days where my shirt has turned red with my own blood from all the bites. But even though they're pests to us, blackflies are important to the ecosystem. They pollinate plants and provide food for dragonflies, fish, and other creatures. For the sake of a healthy ecosystem, I can put up with a few bites every spring.

We had just woken up from one of these short naps when things got weird. Steve, our navigator, told me the compass was wrong. He said it must be broken. Were we lost?

There were no trails and very few landmarks to guide our way. The trees were so close together, sometimes we would get stuck between them. Without the compass, we would risk getting horribly turned around in the dark forest.

I tried to stay calm. A funny thing happens when you are exhausted. You begin to think strange things. Maybe your watch looks like it's telling the wrong time, or your compass seems to be giving you the wrong directions. You stop trusting your gear. Steve was suffering from foggy brain syndrome due to sleep deprivation. So was I, but I had learned to recognize the signs and think my way through the confusion.

While filming *Survivorman*, I'd spent many sleepless nights in the wilderness all over the world. At first this was tough on me, but I learned how to survive on only a few hours of sleep. I discovered that even short, 20-minute naps could make a big difference. But the biggest lesson I learned was to trust my equipment. After all, it wasn't tired like I was!

HOW TO USE A COMPASS

A compass is a device that uses a dial and a needle to show direction. The needle is magnetized, and since the North Pole has the strongest magnetic pull on the planet, compass needles will point toward "magnetic north." Once you know where north is, you can figure out south, east, and west, and use the compass to navigate.

OBSERVE

No compass? No problem! There are many hints you can take from the landscape to figure out direction:

- The predominant winds in *most* parts of North America blow from northwest to southeast. Some trees (white pine, for example), bushes, and grasses will "point" southeast as they lean over in the breeze.

- When you live north of the equator, the sun rises in the east, trails across the south during the day, and sets in the west.

- Moss *tends* to grow on the north side of trees (but beware: it can also grow on the south side of a trunk if the tree lives mostly in the shade).

So I knew the compass was pointing in the right direction. But Steve was arguing that we should go in the opposite direction. He'd convinced himself that the compass was broken. He didn't want to look at it anymore.

Fortunately, Tina and Doug both knew of my ability to think straight on so little sleep. They reassured Steve that I was probably right, and that he should let me lead us out of the thick, bug-infested bush.

Even though I felt woozy, I pointed the compass in the direction it said to go, and we started walking. In a short while, we reached the finish line and discovered that if we had gone the way Steve wanted, we would have headed deeper into the forest and could have become terribly lost.

TRY THIS AT HOME

In addition to figuring out direction, you can use the sun to find out how many hours of daylight are left in a day.

Hold up your arm toward the sun. With your fingers together, bend your wrist so your palm is facing you. Line up your index finger with the bottom of the sun. Now, count how many hand widths (your four fingers) you can fit between the sun and the horizon line (the land). Each hand width equals approximately one hour of daylight.

MISSION ACCOMPLISHED?

Well, kind of. Though we didn't win the race, we were happy to finish without getting lost in the bush. This adventure reminded me to trust in my adventure gear. Unless it's been damaged, a compass will always tell you the truth, even if your foggy brain syndrome is telling you a lie. But it's just as important to observe your co-adventurers.

When I noticed Steve showing signs of foggy brain syndrome, like stumbling around on his feet and saying the same sentence over and over, I knew it was time to step in to avoid what could have been a disastrous decision.

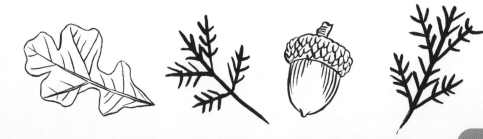

PART THREE:
REACT

LET'S SAY YOU'VE DONE ALL YOU CAN TO PREPARE FOR YOUR ADVENTURE, THEN SOMETHING UNEXPECTED HAPPENS. A tree falls near your tent and rips a hole in the side. You turn right on a trail when you should've turned left. You planned to be home before dark, but you're stuck and you have no flashlight. You've carefully observed the situation to figure out what's going on. Now it's time to *react*.

Whether you start to deal with the situation right away or sit there and do nothing, you are *reacting*. Will you patch your tent, or take a chance that it won't rain overnight? Retrace your steps, or try to find another route back to the trail-head? The choices you make from here on in will determine the outcome of your adventure. These next three stories will show you how I've reacted to dangerous and challenging situations that could happen to any adventurer.

ADVENTURE LOG

LOCATION: The foothills of the Sierra Nevada mountains in California, United States.

CONDITIONS: Dry hills with rocky outcrops and plenty of manzanita trees with abrasive, pokey branches. Sometimes it's easier to crawl on your belly under the trees. But that's where the rattlesnakes are!

GEAR: Signal mirror, tough and durable hiking clothes, whistle.

MISSION: To test out the local search and rescue unit and my own ability to signal for help.

AFTER FOUR DAYS OF SLEEPING ON THE GROUND AND HIKING DEEP INTO THE FORESTS OF THE SIERRA NEVADAS, I WOKE UP WITH BUTTERFLIES IN MY STOMACH. Today was the day! I had arranged for the local search and rescue team to start looking for me on my fifth day in the woods.

These skilled volunteers were all fans of *Survivorman*, so when I'd offered them a chance to hone their skills, they'd jumped at the opportunity to practice locating a lost person: me. They knew I would give them a good challenge.

With dogs and quad bikes, on foot and in airplanes and helicopters, more than 45 people were on their way to find me. How would they spot me in the thick forest? How would I signal to them? If they did see me, would they be able to get to me in this rough terrain? And what would happen if they didn't find me? While they were focused on observation, I knew I had to focus on my ability to react at the first sign of a searcher.

SEARCH AND RESCUE

More than 40,000 people need search and rescue (SAR) in the United States alone every year. I have been a volunteer for search and rescue units in Canada and in the United States, and I am still on call for SAR in Oregon. Almost twice a week, I'll get a text saying that someone is lost and asking for SAR personnel to help find them. It may sound strange to say that it is a lot of fun, but it really is! I get to put my wilderness skills to the test while also helping my community.

Almost as soon as the sun was up, I heard a helicopter. But it seemed to be many miles away. The pilot was flying in a grid-like pattern, searching in a straight line for 1.6 kilometers (one mile), then turning to follow a parallel course for another mile. This way, the searcher in the passenger seat could take a good look at the area below without missing any sections.

REACT

In an emergency or survival situation, the most important thing you can do is make a decision and take action. But acting without considering your options can lead to disaster. Ask yourself these questions *before* you react.

Start with yourself:

- Are you hurt?
- Are you tired or hungry?
- What are you wearing?
- What do you have in your pockets?

Check your immediate surroundings:

- Do you have a tent or other shelter?
- Do you have transportation? (i.e., bicycle, canoe)
- Do you have food, water, or other items in packs?
- What else is nearby—firewood? A swamp full of edible cattails? An all-terrain vehicle with half a tank of gas? How can you use those materials?

Consider the extended area:

- How far are you from safety?
- Which direction is safety, and how difficult will it be to get there?
- What are the challenges to getting to safety, and how can you overcome them?
- Does anyone know you are in trouble, and if so, how long before help arrives?
- How soon can you move, *if* you can move?
- Do you know these answers for sure? (*Not* knowing something is as important to consider as *knowing* something.)

I had prepared by bringing a signaling mirror with me. I observed the forest, noting open areas where I might be visible from overhead. I also listened for the chopper blades, the roar of quad bikes, and barking dogs. But other than the far-off helicopter, I heard nothing.

Then I made a bad decision. I came upon a swampy creek. It was midmorning now, and getting hotter, so I thought it would be safe to wade across the creek—even though I'd get wet up to my waist. I stepped into the water, held my gear over my head, and began to cross. Just then I heard the chopper fly right over me. But I was stuck in the middle of a creek, under a thick tree canopy. This was terrible timing. I considered running after the chopper, but I'd risk injuring myself on the slippery, uneven creek bed. Then I'd be stuck in the forest with a broken ankle or worse. I might have even dropped all my gear into the water. But I had to do *something*. Fast.

TRY THIS AT HOME

Although you can buy special mirrors for signaling, you can use pretty much any mirror or shiny surface.

On a sunny day, head to an open area. Hold the mirror in your right hand and point it at the sun. Stretch your left arm out in front of you. Make a V with your index and middle fingers.

Pick a spot where you want your signal to shine (in a survival situation, this would usually be an airplane or helicopter), and line it up in the middle of your V. Tilt the mirror in your right hand until the reflected light shines at your target, between the two sides of the V.

During my earlier observation, I'd spotted a clearing on the other side of the creek. Staying calm, I moved as swiftly and as safely as I could to the far bank. Have you ever tried to run in water? With slippery rocks underfoot and water plants tangled around my legs, this was not easy.

Back on dry ground, I could pick up my pace without injuring myself. I grabbed my signal mirror, dropped my pack, and sprinted to the clearing.

HOW TO SIGNAL FOR HELP WITHOUT A MIRROR

- Flares can be highly effective, but they don't last long, so don't set them off until you're sure you'll be seen.
- Shine a flashlight the same way you'd shine a mirror (but be mindful of battery power).
- Build a signal fire (remember to make lots of smoke, especially if you're signaling during the day).
- Wear bright-colored clothing to stand out against your surroundings, and tie a rag or piece of clothing to your shelter or nearby branches.
- Make lots of noise, but don't wear out your voice. Clang pots, blow a whistle, or blast an air siren in bursts of three to indicate you need help.

The chopper was gone. *Oh no!* I thought. *I missed my chance.* But all of a sudden, there he was again, and he was about to fly right over me.

This time I was ready. I stood in the open and pointed my signal mirror right at the helicopter. I was trying to reflect the sunlight off the mirror, so I would attract the searcher's attention. Finally, he spotted the flashing mirror. The pilot hovered above me, so close I could see the smile on his face. All he had to do now was radio the rest of the searchers to tell them my location.

No more sleeping on the ground for me!

MISSION ACCOMPLISHED?

Very successfully! The key here was my quick yet safe reaction when I heard the chopper. Crossing the creek wasn't a bad decision at first—I just didn't think I would be up to my hips in water when I heard the searchers coming close. I knew I only had a small window of time to make myself visible.

But if I'd panicked, I could've soaked all my gear or injured myself. Sometimes you have to move slowly, so that you can move quickly later. That strategy worked perfectly for me in the Sierra Nevadas.

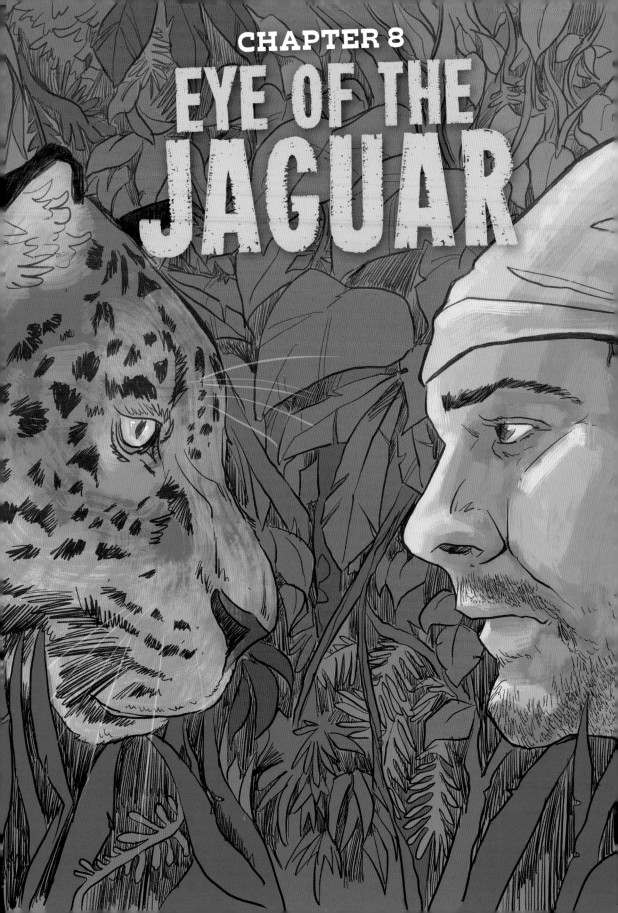

CHAPTER 8
EYE OF THE JAGUAR

ADVENTURE LOG

LOCATION: Amazon rainforest, Ecuador, South America.

CONDITIONS: Hot and wet, with daily downpours that might last six hours.

GEAR: My camera, a machete, a flint striker for starting fires.

MISSION: Make it back to the village without being eaten by a giant cat!

STARING OUT INTO THE DARKNESS OF A JUNGLE CAN BE INTIMIDATING. It's downright terrifying when you spot a pair of eyes staring back at you!

When I became *Survivorman*, I decided one of my first adventures would be in the jungle. I'd been dreaming about it since I was a kid watching Tarzan movies. So I made all the arrangements to film a seven-day survival mission in the Amazon rainforest, packed my bags (and my big boots), and headed to the Waorani nation in Ecuador.

After a long flight in a big jet, followed by a longer flight in a tiny plane, I found myself looking down on a vast stretch of dark green leaves, vines, and plants. Occasionally, I would see big flocks of scarlet macaws. My destination was the head-waters of the Amazon River, which is where the river begins.

The plane landed with a bump on a small strip of grassy field. The Waorani have lived in this area of the Amazon rainforest for thousands of years. I came here with an anthropologist (someone who studies people and cultures) who had been here many times before, and the Waorani welcomed us with big smiles because they knew him so well. Their village, situated beside a rushing jungle river, was made up of seven huts with grass roofs. They showed me how to travel through the jungle, how to catch food, and which plants I could eat. After a few days, they took me far up the river in a dugout canoe and left me alone in the jungle to start my adventure. In my own mind I was pretending to be Tarzan.

I spent six days catching and eating shrimp from the river and trying to keep a fire going in the heavy rain. I managed to avoid the many dangerous creatures that lived there. First there were the snakes, such as the *fer-de-lance*. This snake's deadly bite feels like being stabbed with a red-hot spear. Then there were the huge spiders, stinging bullet ants, wasps as big as my hand, and fuzzy, poisonous caterpillars. The Amazon is also famous for its poison dart frogs. Touching their skin can kill you.

HOW POISONOUS IS A POISON DART FROG?

A single golden poison frog harbors enough poison to kill 10 adults, making these frogs one of the most poisonous animals alive. They are one of many species of toxic frogs known as poison dart frogs. The frogs' poison is found in their skin, making them too toxic to touch. If the golden poison frog's toxin enters your bloodstream, it can kill you in under 10 minutes. While most dart frog species are considered poisonous but not deadly, they are distasteful to many predators, and their poison can cause serious swelling, nausea, and muscular paralysis.

SAFE SLURPING

I had been drinking a *lot* of fresh water on this trip. When there's not much food around, drinking water can trick your stomach into feeling full.

Drinking lots and drinking often are important parts of staying healthy during any adventure. And staying hydrated during a survival ordeal can be a lifesaver. But sometimes, tiny organisms in river or lake water can make you sick.

Boiling water for at least one minute (three minutes at high altitudes) will kill most harmful germs. If the water is dirty or cloudy, make sure to strain it through a cloth before boiling—I have often used a bandana for this.

After surviving these perils, I was feeling relaxed and proud of myself on the last night of my Amazon adventure. Sitting by my fire, I felt the urge to relieve myself. I walked over to my usual "spot" at the edge of my camp, just beyond the light of the fire. Foolishly, I did not check my surroundings. I had been here for six days already. *What other threats could there be?* I thought. I was about to find out there were more dangerous things in the jungle than spiders and snakes.

The jungle looked dark, tangled, and menacing. And there, in that darkness, I saw two red eyes watching me. As the rising moon peeked through the thick jungle canopy, it caused some "eye shine" on a creature lurking in the dark. A shiver ran up my spine when I realized what was staring back at me.

A jaguar.

That's right. While I was casually going to the bathroom, a huge jaguar had snuck up on me. My reaction would make the difference between avoiding this big cat, or being eaten by him.

The jaguar is the third-largest wild cat in the world, after tigers and lions. They can climb trees easily and even like to swim. Their teeth and jaws are powerful enough to break a sea turtle's shell! Jaguars can weigh up to 91 kilograms (200 pounds), which is like 20 house cats. And they have, on occasion, killed and eaten people.

I'm pretty confident when I need to deal with large animals, but this guy was bigger and heavier than me. If he were intent on attacking, I wasn't sure I could fight him off. I knew I shouldn't run because that would trigger his instinct to chase me. But now that he'd found me, it would be too dangerous to spend another night out here. No doubt, he knew I was alone. And I was in *his* territory. I had to get back to the Waorani village. I didn't want to become this big cat's dinner.

I decided to stay calm. I stood tall and whistled loudly to show I was confident and unafraid—and hopefully convince the jaguar I was not easy prey. I had a couple of miles to hike down the small trail to the village. But I had no flashlight. Instead, I used the flip-out LED screen on my camera to light the rough ground. This was going to be a long and scary trek out.

TRY THIS AT HOME

I could spot the jaguar in the dark because his eyes reflected the light of my camera. If you have a dog, take it outside at night with a parent or friend. Bring a flashlight, and have your companion walk the dog about 50 meters (55 yards) away. Point your flashlight in their direction until the dog's eyes light up. If you live near a forest, you can try this trick there, too. Move your flashlight beam around and you might see some little eyes light up. It might be a squirrel, bat, or possum, or maybe even a deer or fox! You don't want to get so close that you light up their whole body; just their eyes. When you get good at this, you can even spot insects this way.

As I hiked away from the big cat, I pointed the dim camera light behind me to see if he was following me. He was! Most big cats are a lot like sharks. They prefer to attack from behind. But that also means looking straight at them with confidence can stop them from thinking you are prey. So every few steps, I turned to look back at him. First, he would be behind my right shoulder and then he would be over on my left. He never stopped watching me. And I never stopped watching him. His cat eyes glowed every time I pointed the camera light his way.

REACT

When I first saw the jaguar, my heart started pounding, and I froze in place. Before I could decide *how* to react to the big cat, my body had its own reaction to the threat. These physical responses help us get ready to react. Here are some of the ways your body might react to fear:

- Your heart will beat faster, and you'll breathe more quickly than usual, to send more oxygen to your muscles—in case you need to run away or fight back.

- Your pupils will dilate (open wider), allowing your eyes to take in extra visual information. This happens so you can keep an eye on your adversary *and* scout for an escape route.

- You'll tense your muscles to get ready for action.

- You might get goose bumps, or feel your hair stand on end. This response is left over from our hairier ancestors. Their long body hair would stand up in stressful situations, to make them look bigger and scarier to predators or other attackers—just like you might see in your pet dog or cat today.

In the dark of the jungle night, I even talked to the jaguar. I told him he didn't need to attack me and that I was his friend. I told him to relax and go find himself something else to eat. I also used another trick. I acted big and strong to signal that I might be tougher than him and maybe he should leave me alone. Sometimes pretending you have courage, even when you don't, can get you through a difficult and scary situation.

After struggling and sweating and tripping my way along the tiny trail, I made it back to the village, which was surrounded by a tall fence to keep the jaguars out. I slipped inside the gate and caught my breath, relieved to be safe. Later that night, in a hut with my Waorani friends, I listened as the jaguar circled the village, letting out little growls. Maybe he understood me when I acted like I wouldn't be a good midnight snack. Or maybe he just wasn't hungry.

MISSION ACCOMPLISHED?

Definitely. Staying out in the jungle all night with the jaguar around might have made me look "tough," but that reaction would've been dangerous and could have resulted in the big cat finally getting curious enough to attack me.

Sometimes it's better to retreat than to fight. This might mean heading home early because the weather is getting bad, or it might mean not pushing my luck when there is a jaguar lurking about. If my mission was to not get eaten by a big jaguar, well, mission accomplished. Whew!

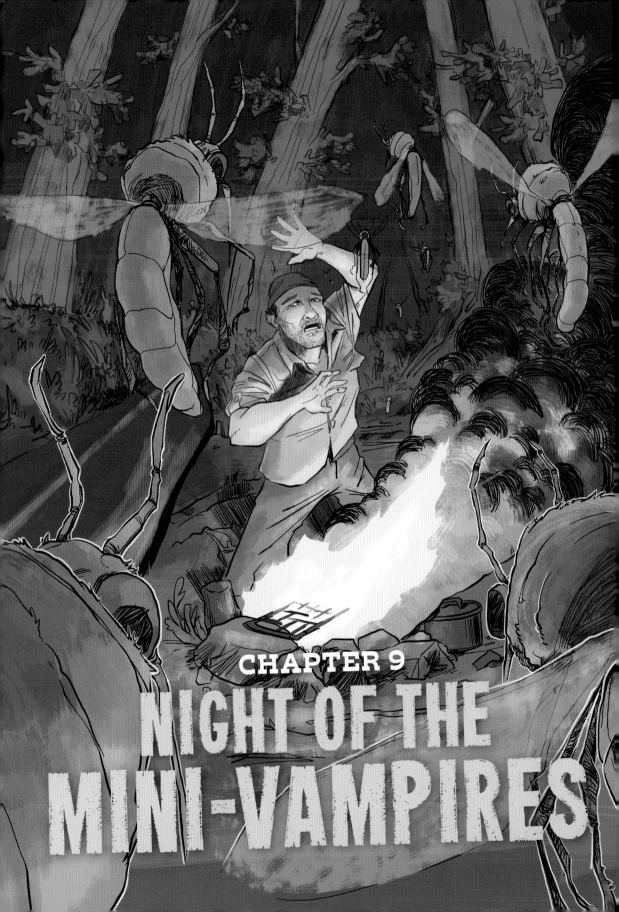

CHAPTER 9
NIGHT OF THE
MINI-VAMPIRES

ADVENTURE LOG

LOCATION: Petawawa River, Ontario, Canada, a beautiful waterway surrounded by green forests and rocky hills and cliffs.

GEAR: Canoe, mosquito screen, fishing gear.

CONDITIONS: Springtime. Early in the evening, right before bed. Quiet and calm—too calm. I could hear every sound in the forest, and that's not always a good thing.

MISSION: Set up camp before getting eaten alive by bloodsucking pests!

I CALL IT THE 10-MINUTE WARNING. Sometimes you can even hear it coming from across a lake. It's a strange and eerie hum. More like a whine than a moan. Something out there is getting ready to hunt. Then they're upon you, and it's a full-on attack!

So far, my day had gone well. The winds had been light as I paddled my canoe down a slow-moving section of the river. I had watched gray jays, bald eagles, a peregrine falcon, a moose, and one of the largest members of the weasel family—a fisher—engaged in their own kind of survival near the banks of the river. I was even able to catch a big fish. A smallmouth bass. It made for a tasty meal as I stretched out on the ground beside my fire.

The sweet-smelling cedar smoke drifted past my nostrils and curled around my canoe, which was turned on its side behind me in case it rained. I was using it as my shelter. The canoe also reflected the heat from the fire back onto my body, keeping me warm.

I stared up into the darkening sky, my belly full of fresh cooked fish, and counted the stars as they appeared.

Loons are part of a family of birds known as divers. Loons spend most of their lives in the water, where they love to eat small fish, crayfish, insect larvae, and sometimes water plants. Loons are especially known for their beautiful and haunting calls—often heard in the middle of the night, echoing across the lake under a full moon and a sky full of stars. When they grow up, loons find a mate and stay together for life.

As I listened to the beautiful call of a loon, I noticed another sound joining in. It started off low and grew louder with each passing minute. My heart began to pound. Something out there was warming up its body temperature, so it could begin to fly.

First there was one, then two, then 10 or 12, then dozens . . . until finally hundreds of them had come to feast on my blood.

Mosquitos!

A mosquito bite or two may be no big deal. But being swarmed by thousands can make you feel sick. Most of us get itchy, red welts from mosquito bites. But some people can suffer more serious allergic reactions.

The worst issue for me would be suffering through an all-night attack. If I didn't react quickly, I could get little to no sleep because I would be swatting mosquitos all night long. That would set me up to have a horrible day without a well-rested mind—something I was going to need to make good decisions while traveling in the remote wilderness. I had only three lines of defense and no time to waste!

REACT

If you're swarmed by mosquitos, your first reaction might be to run around swatting them. But mosquitos are attracted to carbon dioxide, which is what we exhale when we breathe out. The more you run and swat, the more breath you exhale, exciting and attracting even more bugs. Getting a hundred mosquito bites is like getting poison ivy or poison oak. The itch can last for days and torment you endlessly. And just like poison ivy, the worst reaction you can have is to do exactly what you really want to do: scratch! Scratching only makes the welts bleed and can cause a serious infection.

Step 1: I placed some rotten, damp logs on top of the dry burning ones. Most flying insects don't like smoke. The fire would keep these damp logs smoldering, and the smoke would be thick enough to scare off some of the mosquitos.

Step 2: I ran down to the river and smeared mud on my face and neck. Mosquitos can't stick their sucking proboscis through the mud once it dries on your skin.

Step 3: I pulled my mosquito screen out of my pack. Luckily, I'd remembered to bring it. I weighed one end down on top of the canoe and the other on the ground to create a tent-like room around me. I hid under my canoe, trying to sleep, while a million mosquitos made it sound like I was lying beside a six-lane highway.

SURVIVORMOSQUITO?

Even mosquitos have to deal with tough conditions in the wilderness. They are cold-blooded and prefer temperatures that are more than 27°C (80°F), which is why they make that humming sound. They warm up their bodies by buzzing their wings while sitting on blades of grass. At temperatures of less than 10°C (50°F), mosquitos shut down for the winter. The adult females of some species find holes, where they wait for warmer weather, while others lay their eggs in freezing water and die. But with the ability to lay up to five clutches of 100 eggs each, those mama mosquitos are ensuring future generations will be there to swarm the next unsuspecting paddler.

EVEN MOOSE HATE MOSQUITOS!

Have you ever wondered why moose spend so much time submerged in the swamp mud and pond waters? Often, it's simply to escape the biting insects like mosquitos. Moose have been seen running frantically through the bush to escape the bugs.

To keep my fire going, I took one more step. I placed my firewood close to my shelter, so I only had to reach one hand out from under the screen to put a log on the fire when it started to burn low. In those few seconds, however, the mosquitos hovering nearby tried to get in a bite or two.

I have been all around the world and suffered through the worst of the flying and biting insects. The relentless sand gnats in the deserts. Wasps in the Amazon jungle. The deadly malaria-carrying mosquitos of Papua New Guinea. But I will always claim that the Canadian North in the spring has the toughest bugs of all.

TRY THIS AT HOME

Unlike humans, bats *love* mosquitos—some species may eat up to 1,000 bugs in a single night! You can encourage bats to live in your area by putting up bat boxes on the outside of your house. Like bird-houses, these are easily made or purchased from any hardware or nature store. Bat populations are struggling around the world and can use all the help we can give them.

In the middle of the night, I was awakened by the mosquito screen gently tickling my face as the breezes blew it around. From that moment on, I knew all would be well. These new breezes would force the mosquitos back into the trees and away from me. Tomorrow would be another wonderful day in the wilderness.

MISSION ACCOMPLISHED?

Yep! Having a full tool kit of survival skills allowed me to jump into action as soon as I heard the mosquitos coming. I had spent years testing bug repellents and wilderness methods, like smoky fires, to figure out how to beat the biting insects. So I knew how to hide from them and fend off their onslaught.

Learning how to deal with a situation before you face it can help you react quickly and effectively when it does happen to you!

PART FOUR:
ADAPT

YOU'VE PREPARED FOR YOUR ADVENTURE, OBSERVED YOUR SURROUNDINGS, AND REACTED TO UNEXPECTED SITUATIONS. Now it's time to adapt. Things aren't always going to go your way, and you can't always fix a bad situation. Sometimes you just have to follow through and carry on.

To adapt is to continue on, either to a safer situation or to the next part of your adventure. We adapt by shrugging our shoulders and saying, "Oh well." We adapt by bearing down and pushing forward against a harsh wind. We adapt by being inventive and thinking of a new solution to our problems. We even adapt by walking away and starting something new altogether. Learning to adapt to new situations isn't only an adventure or survival skill—it's also something we do every day. And now you need to adapt by turning the page!

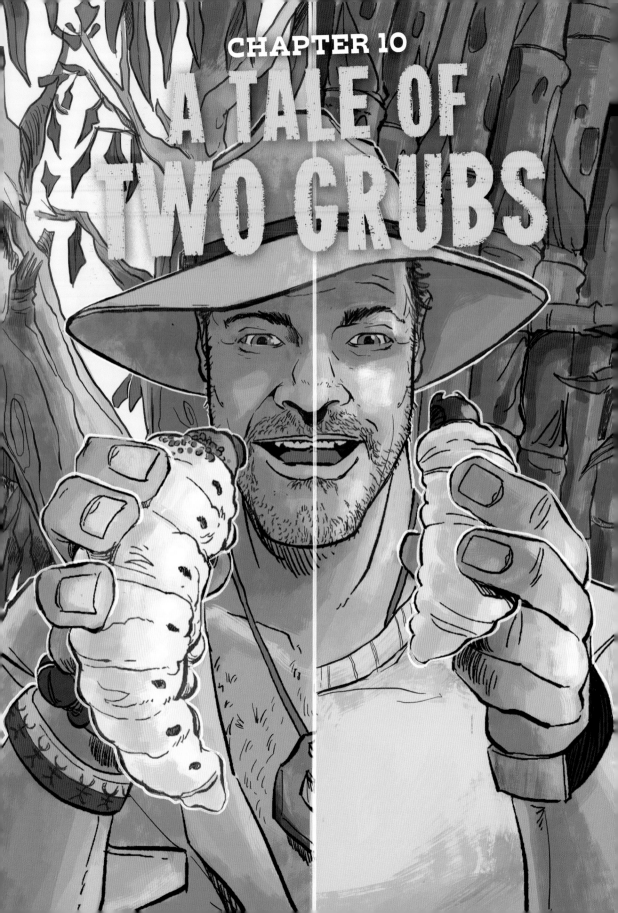

ADVENTURE LOG

LOCATION: This story takes place in two locations, thousands of miles apart—the Australian outback and the island of Siberut in Sumatra, Indonesia.

CONDITIONS: In Australia, it was hot and dry. Flies would land on my cheeks and drink the tears from the corners of my eyes. They weren't biting flies, and after a while they didn't even bother me. In Siberut, it was hot and wet! Some leeches here will burrow under your skin, which can cause serious medical problems. It poured rain almost daily.

GEAR: Machete, big rubber boots, leg gaiters for leech protection.

MISSION: Chow down on two grubs that looked like they could be twins . . . except one was delicious, and the other was one of the most disgusting, make-you-want-to-throw-up kinds of creepy-crawly I'd ever tasted.

IT WAS THE BEST OF GRUBS. IT WAS THE WORST OF GRUBS.

How could two creatures that looked so alike taste completely different? Well, for one, they were in two completely different parts of the planet.

I was filming an episode of *Survivorman* in the Australian outback (pictured above). This was a survival mission, so I didn't have any food. But before I set out, some local people had taught me about a tree called an acacia, or a black wattle. Hidden inside the acacia tree is a delicious critter— not that you'd know that from looking at it. It is about as long as a hot dog and creamy white in color, with a big ugly head. This creature is the larva of a moth, and it is called the witchetty grub.

I spent many hours crawling around acacia trees looking for my first clue: a tiny bit of brown dust, in a tiny pile, on top of brown leaves on brown ground. This dust—made by the grub chewing a hole into the trunk up above—is nearly impossible to spot.

Finally, I found the dust and traced an imaginary line from the pile straight up to the tree. That line led me to a small gray bump in the trunk. In that bump hid the witchetty grub.

My next move was to chop a hole about the size of a marble at the bottom of this little gray mound. I had to work quickly because these grubs can be fast. As soon as I hit the tree, the grub would feel the chop and start chewing a path into the center of the tree. Once I made the hole, I took a long wire, much like a coat hanger, bent the end into a hook, and gently pushed it into the hole. Soon I felt something soft and squishy. The grub!

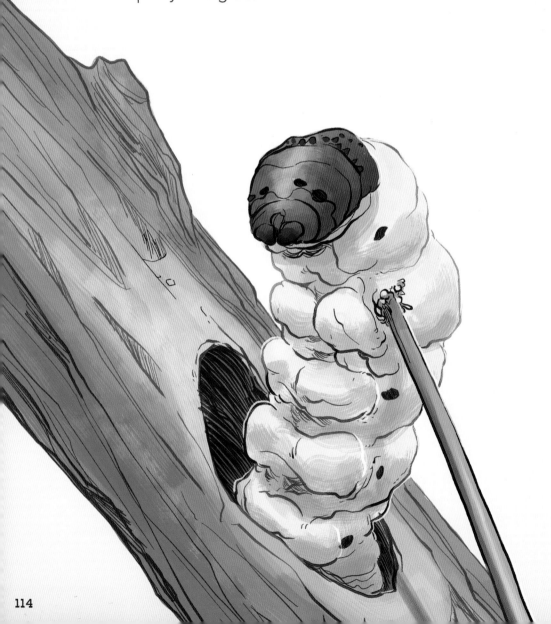

I pushed up a bit farther until I felt a pop. I'd hooked the grub. Carefully, I pulled out this long, creepy larva.

I roasted the witchetty grub over the coals of my fire. The skin tasted like fried chicken, and the insides tasted like scrambled eggs! Mmmm.

But not every wilderness food brings a smile to my face while I munch. Sometimes adapting my diet is not as easy as it was in the Outback. Across the ocean from Australia, on an island called Siberut, I came face-to-face with a worm that tasted nothing like the delicious witchetty grub.

I had been learning survival techniques from a tribe called the Mentawai, and at the end of my training, they wanted to share their favorite treat with me. It's called a sago worm, or the larva of the capricorn beetle. My hunt for this new grub meant searching in the dark and wet jungle for big rotting logs lying on their sides.

ADAPT

On Siberut, the Mentawai people still live a jungle life, hunting with bows and arrows, and trying not to let leeches burrow into their skin. My favorite memory of my time on this island is sitting under huge leaves, staying dry while the rain poured down. I sat there with a shaman (a spiritual leader), and we sang shaman songs together, alone in the jungle.

SIBERUT LEECHES

These little land leeches are so intent on getting blood from their prey that they have not one but two suckers—one on each end of their wiggly body! They hang off plants and wave their heads in the air, sniffing out prey that they can attach to, like you or me, as we walk by and brush against them. I knew they must be dangerous when my Mentawai hosts would run over and pull them off my arms immediately if one got on me.

TRY THIS AT HOME

When I was a kid I was very picky eater, but I learned to enjoy (or at least try) all kinds of food as I got older. Here are some tips for trying an unfamiliar food—maybe even something that grosses you out:

- Take a big breath in and let it out again. Feel courage grow inside you. Lots of people eat and *like* this food.

- Start with small, slow bites to see if you can come to like it. It helps if you are extra hungry when you do this.

- If small bites don't work, close your eyes and pop the food in your mouth. I did this once with scorpions. I roasted them over a fire and popped the crunchy beasts (without the stingers) into my mouth. To my surprise, they tasted great!

Who knows, what you try might one day become your favorite snack.

With my machete, I chopped into the muddy, wet logs until I found the sago worm. It was a lot easier to find than the witchetty grub, but I wasn't sure I was going to be happy about that. This worm was meaner. It tried to bite me with its big, log-eating teeth, so I had to pop off its head with my fingers. Then, with its body still wriggling around, I popped the whole grub into my mouth to eat alive—just as the Mentawai had instructed me to do!

And that's when the taste hit me. Imagine if you poured milk into a small plastic bag. Then you left that bag out in the hot sun for three weeks. And then you had to bite through the plastic to eat the old milk inside. Yeah, I know. I think I will finish this story right here, so I can go throw up.

MISSION ACCOMPLISHED?

Unfortunately, for my taste buds, yes. If you don't usually eat big worms for breakfast, the witchetty grub and the sago worm might not sound like tasty treats. And one definitely wasn't!

You might be wondering why I'd agree to eat something so gross-looking at all. But when you're hungry and alone in the jungle, adapting your eating habits to what is available is a matter of survival. And as disgusting as the sago worm was to me, it was important to honor and respect my Mentawai hosts, who had taught me so much.

When we travel the world and experience other people's cultures, adapting to unfamiliar ways of life can be a way to honor their hospitality. Sometimes that can be easy, like in Australia. When I returned from my adventure there, I let my guides and survival teachers know that I had made a big feast of grubs and enjoyed every last bite.

It was tougher to adapt to my hosts' expectations on the island of Siberut. With the whole tribe watching me, all I could do was swallow the worm down as fast as I could. Once I saw the big smiles on their faces, I knew I had accomplished my mission.

ADVENTURE LOG

LOCATION: Papua New Guinea, a hot island country with huge cliffs covered in dark green moss, high waterfalls, rushing rivers, and plenty of jungle.

CONDITIONS: It rains so hard here that the drops bounce off the ground and make you wet from underneath! If you tried to climb up one of the many steep jungle hills, you'd likely end up slipping back down on wet mud.

GEAR: Machete, big rubber boots, rain gear.

MISSION: Survive a major case of homesickness on an empty stomach, while filming in the New Guinea jungle.

I *LOVE* JUNGLES. THE ONE IN PAPUA NEW GUINEA IS NO EXCEPTION. But halfway through my survival adventure, I was exhausted and hungry. And that brought me down emotionally. I had not been able to find any food for four days, and my situation was about to get worse. It started to rain. And rain. And rain. It was raining so hard that it sounded like a freight train. I couldn't hear myself think. I curled up under the shelter I'd made, but the rain bounced off the ground and sprayed onto me. *Oh well*, I thought. *Not much I can do but try to sleep.* Even if I could find food in this downpour, which would be unlikely, the hunger had sapped all my energy.

As I slept under a roof of big green leaves, I began to dream. Being hungry can give you strange dreams. I dreamt I was in my backyard at home. It was a beautiful sunny day. The grass was green. I was playing with my kids on the swing set. My dog was running around us, barking with joy. My son, who was only three years old, ran over and jumped into my arms, giggling with delight. His little fingers reached up to tickle my cheek.

I woke up suddenly and discovered I was still curled up in the jungle, on the other side of the planet from my family, with my face in a puddle of mud. Oh, and that feeling of my son touching my cheek? That turned out to be a huge jungle cockroach crawling across my face to keep himself out of the mud.

It wasn't just the hunger that made this adventure—and waking up from those dreams—hard. Going with very little food, very little sleep, and very little water are all difficult. But surviving is made tougher when you are completely alone. There is no one to tell your fears to, and no one to share the workload. You have to make every decision, right or wrong, by yourself. You have no choice but to adapt.

DREAM ADVENTURES

When you sleep, your body cycles between REM and non-REM sleep. REM stands for rapid eye movement. During REM sleep, your eyes move rapidly in different directions. The REM cycle is the time when all your dreaming happens, just like my dreams in the jungle. Many artists find inspiration in their dreams. Some inventors keep a notebook beside their bed, so they can write down exciting new ideas they dream about. Try putting a notebook and pencil beside your bed at night. When you wake up in the morning, write down what you remember from the dreams you had. You might invent something special or come up with a wonderful poem or short story!

ADAPT

There are more than 4,000 different kinds of cockroaches in the world, and many that live today are bigger than their ancestors from millions of years ago. The giant burrowing cockroach, from Australia, can grow up to 7.6 centimeters (three inches) long. When it comes to adapting, cockroaches are pretty tough survivors themselves. Though the claim that they would survive a nuclear bomb is likely a myth, cockroaches can endure five times more radiation than humans.

I have been chased by animals and bitten by lots and lots of mosquitos in the wilderness. I have even cut through ice to swim in a lake during the wintertime! But some of the toughest challenges I've faced on my adventures have been emotional, not physical. I can adapt to hunger by finding food. I can adapt to different temperatures by wearing the proper clothing. I can adapt to bad weather by making good shelters. But feeling lonely or helpless requires adapting on the *inside*, rather than the outside. When I'm overtired I can get sad or angry. When I'm in trouble I sometimes struggle with who or what I should blame. But who or what is to blame will never matter. All that matters is what I choose to do next. Because that choice is mine to make.

So I picked myself up off the muddy ground and gave myself a shake. I thought of some small things that would make me feel better—like staying out of the rain. I gathered leaves and branches to make my shelter more watertight. Staying busy is often the answer to dealing with the tough emotions that can come with adventuring. Getting lots of sleep is important, too—even if it means having some weird dreams!

TRY THIS AT HOME

Have you ever watched squirrels or chipmunks make their nests? They pile up forest debris like leaves, branches, and ferns. A big pile of leaves acts the same as a big fluffy sleeping bag, keeping in your body heat. I have even made a quick debris shelter and discovered that it was *too* warm.

Here's how to make this easy shelter:

1. With some friends or family, rake up leaves until the pile is as high as your shoulders.

2. From about half a meter (two feet) off the ground, wiggle into the pile feetfirst, all the way to your shoulders.

3. Notice how fast you start to warm up. You are inside your very own leaf sleeping bag!

MISSION ACCOMPLISHED?

For sure. Adapting to emotional experiences is as key to survival as knowing how to navigate or build a shelter. Even on the best adventures, you might experience a moment of fear or anger.

When I woke up from that dream, I was so sad, I could've cried. And you know what? Sometimes I have cried! It's okay to express my emotions by crying, shouting, or laughing. But I adapted by shedding those emotions, taking some deep breaths, and reminding myself of all the things I could do to improve my circumstances. I would rather be busy than sad.

CHAPTER 12
THE COLDEST NIGHT OF THE YEAR

ADVENTURE LOG

LOCATION: A sparkling, frozen lake beside a snowy black spruce forest in Wabakimi Provincial Park, Ontario, Canada.

GEAR: Rock and steel for fire-starting, layered winter clothing (a base layer next to my skin, a second light layer over that, a thick fleece sweater, and an insulated pair of winter snow pants and winter coat), my camera.

CONDITIONS: How cold is -46°C (-50°F)? So cold that if you poured a glass of water on the ground and bent down to touch it, the water would be frozen by the time your fingers hit the ice!

MISSION: Make sure I don't become a human icicle while filming a winter survival expedition for the first time!

THE FLOAT PLANE "WAVED" GOODBYE WITH A WING DIP AS IT HEADED BACK TO ITS AIR BASE DOZENS OF MILES AWAY. I stood on the frozen lake and watched it get smaller and smaller. Now, I was truly alone. The only sound was the brisk breeze blowing across the ice. It was a bright, sunny day, but it was downright frigid. There would be no casual standing around to figure out what to do. I was wearing good, thick winter clothing, but that wouldn't be enough to survive out here.

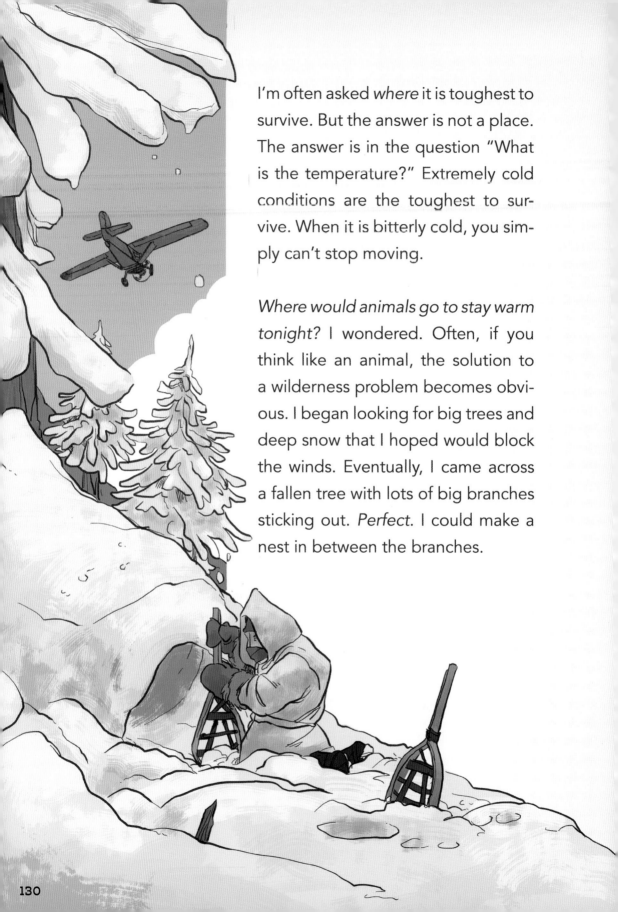

I'm often asked *where* it is toughest to survive. But the answer is not a place. The answer is in the question "What is the temperature?" Extremely cold conditions are the toughest to survive. When it is bitterly cold, you simply can't stop moving.

Where would animals go to stay warm tonight? I wondered. Often, if you think like an animal, the solution to a wilderness problem becomes obvious. I began looking for big trees and deep snow that I hoped would block the winds. Eventually, I came across a fallen tree with lots of big branches sticking out. *Perfect.* I could make a nest in between the branches.

I couldn't change the temperature, so I would have to adapt to my surroundings and make use of what was already here to protect myself *from* the cold temperatures. Just like animals do!

Spruce are part of a family of trees called conifers, and their needles stay on year-round. They don't fall off like other trees' leaves do in the fall. And those needles make great insulation! Whenever possible, I try to make my spruce "mattress" at least one meter (three feet) thick. Anything thinner than that, and by the middle of the night I have flattened them so much that I can see—and feel—the cold ground beneath me. Spruce needles also make a tasty tea full of vitamin C.

It took me a few hours to dig a cave in the snow beside the tree trunk using my snowshoes—a great trick if you don't have a shovel. The snow was over my head—more than 1.8 meters (six feet) deep—so it made a great wind break. Then I gathered green boughs from nearby spruce trees and covered the cave with them. I also laid some boughs on the cave floor. These would be my "mattress."

Before this all starts to sound too cozy, remember that it was getting down to -46°C (-50°F) that night. That kind of cold could penetrate the walls of my shelter and my thick winter clothes. I wouldn't make it through the night without a fire beside me, too. Luckily, I had practiced this advanced skill and knew I could do it safely.

SHELTER FIRES

Knowing how to build a shelter that can safely contain a fire is an advanced skill that can save your life. It's not easy, and it takes a lot of practice to make a safe fire inside a shelter. If you do it wrong, you can burn your shelter down and risk injury or smoke inhalation. Always get an adult's help or supervision before you try building any type of fire.

ADAPT

The shelter I made in the Wabakimi forest is similar to the type of shelter a bear would make for hibernation. While many bears dig their caves right into the earth, some—usually the big males—don't look for a place to spend the winter until well after the first snows come. Those bears would have to adapt the same way I did, by making a cave under a fallen tree. Many bears spend the colder months in a deep, deep sleep, staying alive off fat stored in their bodies. The insulated shelter holds their own bear body heat inside, keeping them warm.

As I dug out a spot for my fire, I found a surprise. Under all that snow were a bunch of rocks—six in total. They were about the size of softballs. *Aha!* I knew exactly what I could do with them.

LOTS OF WAYS TO GET COLD

Our bodies adapt to changes in temperature through a process called thermoregulation. Knowing how and why you're getting cold can help you figure out the best way to get warm.

- **Convection** happens when air or water moves across your skin, taking your body heat with it. That's one of the reasons clothes help us stay warm: they can block the wind and keep your warmth close to your body.

- When your body touches something cold, like the frozen ground, heat leaves your body through **conduction**. Similar to that is **immersion**, such as if you jumped into an ice-cold lake.

- **Radiation** is one of the main ways our bodies lose heat in cold weather. Just like a fire lets off heat, heat leaves our bodies naturally in infrared light (invisible energy) waves.

- As I learned during my slide down a Norwegian mountain (see Chapter 1), you can get cold pretty fast when your skin is wet from rain or sweating. The process of water turning into vapor is called **evaporation**.

I started my fire and spent a couple hours sitting by it to stay warm. I was surrounded by deep snow, a thick forest of trees, and my own bush shelter, but I knew that as the temperature dropped, my nice big fire would feel no warmer than a small candle. I needed another source of heat. Time for the rocks! I placed them around the edges of the firepit, turning them every so often so they would get warm on all sides.

TRY THIS AT HOME

On a cold night at home or a chilly night out camping, ask an adult to help you fill up a rigid plastic water bottle (like a Nalgene) with hot water. Now put the bottle inside your sleeping bag with you, and it will keep you warm all night long! If you find yourself chillier than you expected on a camping trip and you didn't pack one of those rubber hot water bottles, then this is a neat trick.

As I was getting sleepy, I picked up the heated rocks. They weren't so hot that I couldn't pick them up—closer to the temperature of a hot water bottle. And that was exactly how I wanted to use them. I put the rocks against my legs and stomach and felt their warmth through my winter pants. I even put one inside my coat. These were "rock-hot water-bottles"!

For the rest of the night I slept peacefully, as if I were snug in bed in a warm house, while right outside my little shelter the wind howled, the snow blew around, and the cold temperatures froze everything else in sight.

MISSION ACCOMPLISHED?

Absolutely! You can die of exposure to the cold in temperatures like this. Not only did I survive, but I also actually got some sleep inside my bush shelter—a tough thing to do on such a freezing night.

I couldn't change the frigid conditions, but I could adapt to them by making good use of the materials around me. I used the snow, the fallen tree, the spruce boughs, and those rocks to keep myself warm throughout the night.

EPILOGUE TO ADVENTURE

A LONG TIME AGO, WHEN I WAS ABOUT YOUR AGE, I REALLY WANTED TO EXPERIENCE NATURE AND ADVENTURE. I wanted to talk to the animals and take pictures of them. I wanted to know what plants I could eat and how to start a safe fire. I wanted to climb mountains, paddle rivers, hike trails, and stay outside overnight with friends—and on my own.

I watched every TV show I could find about nature and the outdoors. These days, I can do that research online, too. I read adventure stories and I combed through guidebooks. I would stare out my windows watching birds in the trees and squirrels gathering nuts. I didn't care if it was the worms in my backyard, or the deer I could spot down by the creek; if it was a part of nature, I was interested. Maybe you are like me. Maybe you find birds or insects or big animals or trees or forests exciting. Maybe you like playing video games, and you want to go on your own adventure *for real*. Maybe you like playing sports, but you want to test your strength in new ways. Maybe you love to study. Well, in nature there are endless things to study!

As I grew up, I realized I wanted to travel to far-off places and tell stories about nature in films and on television. I wanted to explore and challenge myself in remote jungles and on the sides of mountains. I started small by learning simple wilderness techniques from books, TV, and anyone who would teach me. Then I took courses in skills like canoeing and rock climbing and even dog sledding! I never stopped thinking about who I wanted to be and what I wanted to do.

Nature is all around you. It is right outside your window, even if that window is 40 floors up in the middle of a big city. I have a thousand tales to tell of wilderness adventure because I have been going outside for many years. But your adventure can start in your own backyard or down the street. It can start on the other side of town or city or at the end of a not-too-long car ride. You can learn about nature and animals by building bat houses or sitting by a creek for an hour. Your passport is a good pair of shoes, a jacket, and a survival kit. You might also want to bring along some good friends or your parents. Or you may want to find a good outdoor guide to tag along with. Guidebooks on wildlife, birds, trails, insects, fish, trees, and plants are easy to find, and they are a great way to get you excited about adventures that may lie ahead.

The more time you spend in nature, the more comfortable you will become. You don't need to be alone in the middle of a jungle to experience the outdoors, but developing your wilderness skills and spending time outside can open up possibilities for future adventures. Your parents, other adults, or outdoor teachers of all kinds can help show you how to have fun in nature safely.

I want your wilderness dreams to come true. Your first adventure can start with one simple action. Go outside. What are you waiting for? Let's go adventuring!

SPECIAL THANKS

To my wife, Caroline, for giving me inspiration just by walking into the room. (And whom I miss when she leaves the room.)

To my kids: Raylan and Logan, you are a continued source of intense pride and love for me, and I am thrilled you are now taking your own great adventures!

To Terry McManus for never ceasing to believe in me and for somehow thinking I had talent (well, at least I think you thought that!).

And to Claire Caldwell, who edited this book. I have never had such wonderful, creative, and talented (and patient) attention to detail given to my work. This is your book as much as it is mine.

ACKNOWLEDGMENTS

The mentors in my life came mostly from books, TV shows, and films. Yet they still managed to shape my life of adventure, and I am forever grateful. Filmmakers such as Jacques Cousteau and Bill Mason inspired me to pick up a camera and film scenarios no one had ever filmed before. A host of adventurers and outdoors people have inspired me and given me heights to reach for, and they include: Rob Stewart, Archie Belaney (aka Grey Owl), Hap Wilson, Wendy Grater, Keith Blisset, Dave Halladay, Bob Groves, Fred Rowe, David Arama, and the incomparable Doug Getgood. There are fictional (and fantastical) characters who have teased my imagination and helped me to dream, and they include Grey Owl (aka Archie Belaney), Jeremiah Johnson, and Tarzan. And finally, there are artists and creators and adventurers who continue to focus on creating and achieving throughout their whole lives. They inspire me, and they are: Bruce Cockburn, Robbie Robertson, Clint Eastwood, Frank Zappa (RIP), Martin Scorsese, Margaret Atwood, Caroline's Boppi, and well, basically, anyone out there who is over the age of 60 or 70 or 80 or 90 and continues to contribute to society, to humans, to life, in order to better this little planet and those of us on it. Special thanks to Laura Bombier, whose ability behind the lens is unsurpassed when it comes to photographing the heart of a subject (and who is responsible for many of the wonderful photos in this book).

FURTHER READING

Angier, Bradford. *How to Stay Alive in the Woods: A Complete Guide to Food, Shelter and Self-Preservation . . . Anywhere.* New York: Black Dog & Leventhal, 2012.

Bickel, Lennard. *This Accursed Land.* Sydney: Bloomsbury Reader, 2015.

Herrero, Stephen. *Bear Attacks. Their Causes and Avoidance.* 3rd ed. Guilford, CT: Lyons Press, 2018.

Kochanski, Mors L. *Northern Bushcraft.* Auburn, WA: Lone Pine Publishing, 1991.

Logan, Richard D. and Tere Duperrault Fassbender. *Alone: A Fascinating Study of Those Who Have Survived Long, Solitary Ordeals.* Green Bay, WI: TitleTown Publishing, LLC, 2010.

McPherson, John and Geri. *Primitive Wilderness Skills, Applied & Advanced.* Randolph, KS: Prairie Wolf, 1996.

Olsen, Larry Dean. *Outdoor Survival Skills.* 6th ed. Chicago: Chicago Review Press, 1997.

Owl, Grey. *The Collected Works of Grey Owl.* Toronto: Prospero, 1999.

Peterson, Lee. *A Peterson Field Guide to Edible Wild Plants: Eastern and Central North America.* Boston: Houghton Mifflin Harcourt, 1999.

Pryde, Duncan. *Nunaga: Ten Years of Eskimo Life.* 2nd ed. New York: Bantam Books, 1973.

Stroud, Les. *Survive! Essential Skills and Tactics to Get You Out of Anywhere—Alive.* Toronto: Collins, an imprint of HarperCollins Canada, 2008.

———. *Will to Live: Dispatches from the Edge of Survival.* Toronto: Collins, an imprint of HarperCollins Canada, 2010.

Wescott, David. *Camping in the Old Style.* Layton, UT: Gibbs Smith, 2015.

Wilson, Hap. *Temagami: A Wilderness Paradise.* 2nd ed. Erin, ON: Boston Mills Press, 2011.

IMAGE CREDITS
PHOTO CREDITS

All photography by Laura Bombier, except for the following images:

Chapter 2

22 Two bull moose challenge one another during the fall rut season.
   © Kelp Grizzly Photography / Shutterstock.com

Chapter 4

47 Cattails © Green-fly Media via Creative Market
49 Urban fox scavenging on the edge of parkland in a residential area
   © Jamie Hall / Shutterstock.com
50 Lynx © Byrdyak via Creative Market

Chapter 5

63 Lizard © Byrdyak via Creative Market

Chapter 8

90 Yellow Frog, golden poison dart frog © TeaBerry via Creative Market
93 Jaguar, Panthera Onca, Female © reisegraf.ch via Creative Market

Chapter 9

101 Loon © Siân C Photography via Creative Market

Chapter 11

124 Red-brown Madagascar cockroaches © Sova via Creative Market

ILLUSTRATION CREDITS

All illustrations by Andrew P. Barr, except for the following images:

Bird with open beak (iii); bird with wing stripe (1); seven-lobed branch (1); campfire (7); nine-lobed leaf (29); fan-shaped leaf (29, 83); oval leaf (29, 83); deer (49); goose (49); wolf (49); branch with thin needles (58, 83); double-branched pine needles (58, 107); long branch with leaves (58); asymmetrical leaf (73, 83); longer five-lobed branch (73); shorter five-lobed branch (73); acorn (73, 83); pinecone (107); evergreen (107); 13-lobed branch (131); 17-lobed branch (131); mountains (131); and figure with backpack (138, 145) from Rustic Clipart Designs Vol 2 © BirDIYvia Creative Market

Map (i, iv, 8, 16, 25, 35, back cover); compass (i, iv, 42, 51, 61, 71, back cover); multitool (i, vi, 74, 80, 95, 103, back cover); and campfire (i, vi, 108, 116, 124, 133, back cover) from Hiking and Camping set © Alex Krugli via Creative Market
Seamless topographical map © Pgmart via Creative Market (24)

20 Adhesive tape pieces © amber&ink via Creative Market

Vintage vignette tan paper texture © Lost & Taken